MADE E-Z™
PRODUCTS

Business Letters

Kim Komando

Made E-Z

MADE E-Z PRODUCTS™ Inc.
Deerfield Beach, Florida / www.MadeE-Z.com

Business Letters Made E-Z™
Printed in the United States of America

Published by:
MADE E-Z PRODUCTS 384 South Military Trail
Deerfield Beach, FL 33442

http://www.MadeE-Z.com

1 2 3 4 5 6 7 8 9 10

Business Letters Made E-Z™

Table of Contents

Business Letters by Category

Announcements, Awards, Requests

Apologies, Condolences, Complaints

Performance & Procedure

Human Resources

Account Review Request

TO: [*First and last name of person receiving memo*]

FROM: [YOUR NAME]
[YOUR TITLE]

DATE: [DATE]

SUBJECT: Account Reviews Scheduled

From the very first "Hello," sales is a series of steps leading up to the customer's door. We may have to knock several times—some days loudly, some softly. Once inside, we offer confirmation of our professionalism and evidence that supports our contention that doing business with [YOUR COMPANY NAME] leads to shared success.

The intricacies of the sales cycle warrant maintaining close contact with your customers and management. As your coach, I want to help our team be successful in opening every door and keeping it open to future business.

I have scheduled an account review for you on [*Date of meeting*] at [*Location within office where meeting will be held*] at [*Time the meeting begins*]. Please be prepared to discuss in detail your present, pending, and potential opportunities. In addition, we will discuss quotas and conduct an analysis of business lost. Specifically, list in chart form by customer name the following: [*Describe what you want to know*]. I am most interested in [*Describe the information most important to you*].

If for some reason the account review conflicts with your schedule, advise me in writing immediately. Otherwise, I look forward to hearing all about your stairway to prosperity.

cc: [COPIES TO]

Accountant Review Transmittal

[DATE]

[Mr./Mrs./Ms./Dr.] [FIRST AND LAST NAME]
[TITLE]
[COMPANY]
[ADDRESS]
[CITY], [STATE] [ZIP CODE]

Dear [Mr./Mrs./Ms./Dr.] [LAST NAME]:

Expertise is achieved through continuous education and proficiency. We rely on your judgment and knowledge in reviewing the enclosed records and statements for accuracy and compliance as dictated by the Financial Accounting Standards Board (F.A.S.B.). Therefore, herewith are [*Name of company*]'s accounting records covering the year(s) [*Year(s) of the accounting records*].

[YOUR COMPANY NAME]'s goal in requesting your services is to reach an intelligent decision regarding [*Describe why* COMPANY *is reviewing accounting records*]. Time is of the essence, so we must have this information no later than [*Date information is required*]. After examining the project's scope, please call with an estimated charge for [COMPANY]'s services. Thank you for your assistance in this matter. I always hold your opinions in the highest regard.

Sincerely yours,

[YOUR NAME]
[YOUR TITLE]

Achievement of Promotion

TO: All Staff

FROM: [YOUR NAME]
[YOUR TITLE]

DATE: [DATE]

SUBJECT: [*First and last name of person promoted*]'s Achievements Recognized with Promotion

It gives me great pleasure to acknowledge [*First and last name of person promoted*]'s dedication and hard work with a promotion and change in responsibilities to [*Title of person promoted*]. In this new position, [*First name of person promoted*] will be directing our [*Departmental functions of person promoted*] efforts and is the primary contact for related projects and questions. As in the past, I am sure you will find [*First name of person promoted*] a truly gifted and innovative individual eager to help and to promote our company's growth.

cc: [COPIES TO]

Acknowledgement of Compliment About Employee

[DATE]

[Mr./Mrs./Ms./Dr.] [CUSTOMER'S FULL NAME]
[CUSTOMER'S TITLE]
[COMPANY]
[ADDRESS]
[CITY], [STATE] [ZIP CODE]

Dear [Mr./Mrs./Ms./Dr.] [CUSTOMER'S LAST NAME]:

Customer appraisals carry more weight than management appraisals. You are who we ultimately serve and, therefore, the best source of feedback. Thank you for taking time from your busy schedule to let us know that we are earning high marks with [COMPANY].

Your letter praising [*First and last name of person who received compliment*] was a gracious acknowledgment of our stringent standards and commitment to 100 percent customer satisfaction. I guarantee that your letter will not be sitting on my desk much longer. [*First and last name of person who received compliment*] will receive [YOUR COMPANY NAME] accolades for exemplifying a first rate professional image. Again, thank you for bringing such good news into our company. Your comments prove that hard work and quality never go out of style.

Sincerely yours,

[YOUR NAME]
[YOUR TITLE]

Active Customer Questionnaire

[DATE]

[Mr./Mrs./Ms./Dr.] [CUSTOMER'S FULL NAME]
[CUSTOMER'S TITLE]
[COMPANY]
[ADDRESS]
[CITY], [STATE] [ZIP CODE]

Dear [Mr./Mrs./Ms./Dr.] [CUSTOMER'S LAST NAME]:

Our company's golden rule is simple: treat every customer with the same dignity and respect you would expect if you were the customer. Once a year, we randomly select customers from our files and ask them to tell us how we are doing. This equips our organization to meet the most significant of standards—our customers' standards.

Using a 1 to 10 rating scale, where 1 represents total disagreement and 10 total accord, please answer the seven questions below. Your answers will give us insight into our own operations. When completed, simply drop this letter in the mail using the enclosed self-addressed, stamped envelope.

__ 1. Your staff is always pleasant and helpful.

__ 2. Promised delivery schedules are adhered to.

__ 3. Your products are superior in performance and quality.

__ 4. Your pricing is competitive.

__ 5. It's easy to buy from your company.

__ 6. Your company is responsive to our needs.

__ 7. We plan to be your customer in the future.

In tallying the results, we may contact you for additional information that will help us heed our golden rule. Thank you for taking the time to help us learn how to serve you better.

Sincerely yours,

[YOUR NAME]
[YOUR TITLE]

Adjust Accountant's Bill

[DATE]

[Mr./Mrs./Ms./Dr.] [FIRST AND LAST NAME]
[TITLE]
[COMPANY]
[ADDRESS]
[CITY], [STATE] [ZIP CODE]

Dear [Mr./Mrs./Ms./Dr.] [LAST NAME]:

By now, you've probably noticed that [YOUR COMPANY NAME] is a bottom-line-oriented company constantly checking and double-checking its facts and figures. Although [COMPANY] has done a fine job managing our books and advising us on tax matters, I question the calculations on the latest bill we received. The total amount due is not reasonable, and I'm sure a review will result in a favorable adjustment for [YOUR COMPANY NAME].

[YOUR COMPANY NAME] appreciates our affiliation with [COMPANY], but I cannot justify bills of this nature. You have always handled our statements very professionally, so I ask that you personally analyze this bill and the amount owed to [COMPANY]. Thank you in advance for your assistance. Even the masters are subject to error at times.

Respectfully yours,

[YOUR NAME]
[YOUR TITLE]

Adjust Lawyer's Bill

[DATE]

[Mr./Mrs./Ms./Dr.] [FIRST AND LAST NAME]
[TITLE]
[COMPANY]
[ADDRESS]
[CITY], [STATE] [ZIP CODE]

Dear [Mr./Mrs./Ms./Dr.] [LAST NAME]:

By nature, most people throughout the world are quite alike. Investing in an education gives one a variety of options particularly for the pursuit of specialized professions. I admire your dedication and appreciate the years you spent in school, both of which have enabled you to represent [YOUR COMPANY NAME].

I am, however, inclined to hold you in contempt of court. Frankly, when I looked at the bill for your services regarding [*Describe work performed by* COMPANY], I did a double-take. Perhaps we have simply had a misunderstanding over fees and expenses, or perhaps my records have somehow been confused with those of another client. Regardless, I ask you to review the bill for any possible adjustments and advise me of your position as soon as possible.

I thank you for your professional courtesy in this matter. Off the record, it's no secret that money is tight in our economy. Anything you can do to reduce the total is greatly appreciated.

Respectfully yours,

[YOUR NAME]
[YOUR TITLE]

Advertisement for Employment

[DATE]

[Mr./Mrs./Ms./Dr.] [FIRST AND LAST NAME]
[TITLE]
[COMPANY]
[ADDRESS]
[CITY], [STATE] [ZIP CODE]

Dear [Mr./Mrs./Ms./Dr.] [LAST NAME]:

Financial statements and capital equipment are important, but a professional team builds security and increases profitability. We are increasing our wealth with the addition of hand-picked talent.

Because [COMPANY] targets a qualified audience, please place the following advertisement in your employment classified section under [*Industry or profession category under which advertisement should be placed*]. We would like the advertisement to run [*Dates the advertisement should be put in publication*].

JOIN OUR WINNING TEAM

Our business is growing, and we are seeking quality people with a strong professional work ethic to share in our enthusiasm. Qualified, experienced [*Name of position open for applications*] should apply by [*Describe the actions taken by reader to apply for job*].

Upon receipt of this letter, please telephone with the estimated cost, and we'll arrange payment. Thank you for your assistance in keeping our assets strong.

Sincerely yours,

[YOUR NAME]
[YOUR TITLE]

Advertising Fee Request

[DATE]

[Mr./Mrs./Ms./Dr.] [FIRST AND LAST NAME]
[TITLE]
[COMPANY]
[ADDRESS]
[CITY], [STATE] [ZIP CODE]

Dear [Mr./Mrs./Ms./Dr.] [LAST NAME]:

Business success does not require a Bachelor or Master's degree. Notwithstanding formal education's benefits, companies thrive with an enduring M.A.P. degree. That is, practicing the lessons of Management, Advertising, and Positioning in daily operations.

Taking the "A" from our diploma, I am exploring advertising and promotional efforts for [YOUR COMPANY NAME]. I cannot honestly say I have read every issue of your publication. From what I have seen, however, it appears that we may have a fit between your audience and our customers.

To make my decision, I require the hard facts normally contained in a publication's media kit. This can be sent to me at [YOUR COMPANY NAME's *address*]. Please be sure that the package includes your advertising rates, audience demographic profile, average life span per issue, one sample issue, publication frequency, and circulation data, including a complete breakdown of complimentary and paid subscriptions.

I look forward to receiving [COMPANY]'s literature and making a well-informed decision as another contribution to our company's core M.A.P. curriculum.

Sincerely yours,

[YOUR NAME]
[YOUR TITLE]

Agency Fee Request

[DATE]

[Mr./Mrs./Ms./Dr.] [FIRST AND LAST NAME]
[TITLE]
[COMPANY]
[ADDRESS]
[CITY], [STATE] [ZIP CODE]

Dear [Mr./Mrs./Ms./Dr.] [LAST NAME]:

Marketing without a shrewd advertising plan can be hazardous to a business' health. [YOUR COMPANY NAME] is interested in the services offered by [COMPANY] to help us spread our good word. Before proceeding any further, we would like a little information about your advertising background and success stories.

Please forward to my attention the following materials: company profile, client list, basic fee schedule, and professional references. These can be sent to [YOUR COMPANY NAME's *address*].

We do not require a formal advertising plan now; this can be determined later. However, if you have a general notion of how our account would be handled, by all means jot it down. I look forward to reviewing your firm's package. When I receive the material, I may telephone and set a meeting time because the health of our business is a vital asset.

Sincerely yours,

[YOUR NAME]
[YOUR TITLE]

Aids and Life Threatening Illness

TO: [*First and last name of person receiving the memo*]

FROM: [YOUR NAME]
[YOUR TITLE]

DATE: [DATE]

SUBJECT: AIDS and Other Life-Threatening Illnesses

One cannot read the newspaper or watch television without becoming aware of life-threatening illnesses such as AIDS, cancer, and heart disease. We have become concerned about the debilitating effects such illnesses have on the individual and the community. Unfortunately, people afflicted with life-threatening illnesses are often branded as outcasts and suffer the remainder of their lives in exile.

Education is of utmost importance. [YOUR COMPANY NAME] supports continuing employment of workers with life-threatening illnesses. In accordance with the law and acceptable performance standards, we make reasonable accommodations for employees with life-threatening illnesses. We would like them to keep their jobs as long as possible. Medical information is held in strict confidence, and all regulations prohibiting inappropriate disclosure are enforced.

Life-threatening illnesses do not discriminate in choosing their victims. Any one of us could be next. As always, we encourage and support every [YOUR COMPANY NAME] employee, even those whom society isolates because of their maladies.

cc: [COPIES TO]

Anniversary Announcement

[DATE]

[Mr./Mrs./Ms./Dr.] [CUSTOMER'S FULL NAME]
[CUSTOMER'S TITLE]
[COMPANY]
[ADDRESS]
[CITY], [STATE] [ZIP CODE]

Dear [Mr./Mrs./Ms./Dr.] [CUSTOMER'S LAST NAME]:

Successful personal and professional relationships are cooperative endeavors. This fine day at [YOUR COMPANY NAME] would not be possible without companies like [COMPANY]. I am proud that over the past [*Length of time of* YOUR COMPANY NAME *has been in business*] years, our operation has helped people appreciate the true meaning of customer satisfaction and quality management.

We look forward with confidence; our past success merely hints at the accomplishments we expect to see in the future. Speaking for the entire [YOUR COMPANY NAME] team, we thank you for your support and participation in our growth. The encouragement of [COMPANY] and other fine companies has made it possible for us to mark this momentous occasion.

Sincerely yours,

[YOUR NAME]
[YOUR TITLE]

Announce Annual Meeting of Stockholders

[DATE]

[Mr./Mrs./Ms./Dr.] [FIRST AND LAST NAME]
[TITLE]
[COMPANY]
[ADDRESS]
[CITY], [STATE] [ZIP CODE]

Dear [Mr./Mrs./Ms./Dr.] [LAST NAME]:

Where there is unity, there is victory. [YOUR COMPANY NAME]'s triumph could not have occurred without support in and out of our headquarters halls. I extend my personal invitation to you to make an investment in our future and join [YOUR COMPANY NAME]'s visionary team at our forthcoming annual meeting of shareholders.

On [*Date of annual meeting*], at [*Location of annual meeting*], beginning promptly at [*Time annual meeting begins*], you will hear firsthand [YOUR COMPANY NAME]'s strategies for increased growth and income to promote higher returns on shareholder investment. I encourage your participation in this event, because there are many important issues under discussion and review. Those who are unable to join in this meeting can voice their opinions with the enclosed proxy.

Your completion of the proxy ensures an accurate reflection of our shareholders' thoughts regarding future moves. Should this be your method of participation, please sign, date, and mail the proxy promptly in the envelope provided. Otherwise, complete the information confirming attendance and let your voice be heard at the meeting. On behalf of the Board of Directors and [YOUR COMPANY NAME] employees, I thank you for your assistance in the direction of our company.

Sincerely yours,

[YOUR NAME]
[YOUR TITLE]

Answering the Telephone

TO: [*First and last name of person receiving memo*]

FROM: [YOUR NAME]
[YOUR TITLE]

DATE: [DATE]

SUBJECT: Procedure for Answering the Telephone

You never get a second chance to make a first impression. Therefore, we want to make sure that our business associates and customers get the right impression the first time, and every time, they call [YOUR COMPANY NAME]. A standard greeting creates continuity and helps to maintain a professional image.

Your primary goal during those first few seconds of conversation is to let the caller know that he or she has reached the right place and that you are glad he or she phoned. Your words and tone should be pleasant at all times.

Job responsibilities and organizational roles require different styles when answering the telephone. In your position as [*Job title of first and last name of person receiving memo*], the telephone should be answered during business hours in the following manner: [*Describe the greeting to be used by first and last name of person receiving memo*].

Post this script by your telephone as a reminder of the correct way to answer the telephone. [YOUR COMPANY NAME] wants every business associate and customer to get the right impression of every aspect of our business every time. Thank you for contributing to our professional image.

cc: [COPIES TO]

Apology for Missed Meeting

[DATE]

[Mr./Mrs./Ms./Dr.] [CUSTOMER'S FULL NAME]
[CUSTOMER'S TITLE]
[COMPANY]
[ADDRESS]
[CITY], [STATE] [ZIP CODE]

Dear [Mr./Mrs./Ms./Dr.] [CUSTOMER'S LAST NAME]:

When I was a child, I sometimes had trouble mastering things others picked up with ease. I remember always offering an excuse when I dropped the ball or received a low test score. One day all that changed when my father sat me down on his knee and in a burly tone said, "An excuse is just a statement you make when you know you could have done better."

Today, many years later, I am reminded of his wisdom as I offer no excuse for missing our meeting. I have chastised myself repeatedly for such a display of unprofessionalism. There is no reason good enough, and to give one would be an insult to your intelligence.

I only hope this has not reflected poorly on me or our company. Please accept my apologies and know I would like another chance to set a convenient time for us to meet. Thank you for understanding. You have my promise that this will never happen again.

Sincerely yours,

[YOUR NAME]
[YOUR TITLE]

Application for Credit

[DATE]

[Mr./Mrs./Ms./Dr.] [FIRST AND LAST NAME]
[TITLE]
[COMPANY]
[ADDRESS]
[CITY], [STATE] [ZIP CODE]

Dear [Mr./Mrs./Ms./Dr.] [LAST NAME]:

Believe it or not, success can be trendsetting and conservative simultaneously. Fortitude and wisdom achieve balance between innovation and risk protection. [YOUR COMPANY NAME] continues to master business' scales of justice by developing a healthy market and being, much to our liking, a little set in our ways.

We tip the scales more in the checks and balances tradition. Many other businesses our size probably would have extended themselves with credit already. In fact, I can't tell you how many creditors and suppliers have asked us if we wanted credit.

Today, credit with frequent suppliers like [COMPANY] is the next logical step in furthering growth and streamlining operations. We would like any purchases over a [*Time between invoices, i.e., 30, 60, or 90 days*]-day period totaled and invoiced. The benefits of reduced paperwork and processing hours for our respective organizations are obvious.

Please send a credit application and any other necessary paperwork to [*First and last name of the person at* YOUR COMPANY NAME *responsible for completing credit applications*]. [YOUR COMPANY NAME] is ready for credit now that the market rage we created has left us standing alone on enterprise's center stage.

Sincerely yours,

[YOUR NAME]
[YOUR TITLE]

Application Request

[DATE]

[Mr./Mrs./Ms./Dr.] [CUSTOMER'S FULL NAME]
[CUSTOMER'S TITLE]
[COMPANY]
[ADDRESS]
[CITY], [STATE] [ZIP CODE]

Dear [Mr./Mrs./Ms./Dr.] [CUSTOMER'S LAST NAME]:

There is no way around it. Credit applications are a necessary evil in business. Our last thought is to burden you with additional paperwork, but we require certain information before establishing a credit account for [COMPANY].

Enclosed is [YOUR COMPANY NAME]'s standard credit application. Evaluating your credit request is easier when the application is printed or typed. If you run out of room on any item, simply use a blank page on which you reference the item number(s) to which the details pertain and attach it to the application. One last thing, the signature on the application must be by an authorized [COMPANY] representative.

Please allow us [*Length of time* YOUR COMPANY NAME *needs before responding to* COMPANY] days to process your request. Thank you for your interest in the payment alternatives offered by our company. This is another example of [YOUR COMPANY NAME]'s dedication to tailoring our operations to unique customer requirements.

Sincerely yours,

[YOUR NAME]
[YOUR TITLE]

Appointment Request Decline

[DATE]

[Mr./Mrs./Ms./Dr.] [FIRST AND LAST NAME]
[TITLE]
[COMPANY]
[ADDRESS]
[CITY], [STATE] [ZIP CODE]

Dear [Mr./Mrs./Ms./Dr.] [LAST NAME]:

Time management is a science. Glancing at my calendar each morning, I am reminded how much effort is required to squeeze 20 hours of labor into an 8- to 12-hour workday. Too much time spent in one place or too little in another upsets the balance.

Knowing this should help you understand why I must decline your request for a meeting. I never make a commitment unless I am sure I can keep it. Broken promises damage professional reputations.

Until we can set a time during which I can be certain that nothing will pre-empt our appointment, there is an alternative. I trust you had a specific purpose in mind when requesting the meeting. Therefore, feel free to send any documentation or literature you wanted to present in person. Thank you for your professional courtesy. I look forward to receiving the information.

Sincerely yours,

[YOUR NAME]
[YOUR TITLE]

Appraisal of Performance Meeting

TO: [*First and last name of person receiving memo*]

FROM: [YOUR NAME]
[YOUR TITLE]

DATE: [DATE]

SUBJECT: Performance Appraisal Meeting

Action and planning are essential components of a successful career. Implementing one without the other is a futile, often frustrating, experience for the organization and employee. While we do our best to encourage informal discussions on important topics, this casual approach does not provide the opportunity for in-depth reviews.

We consider formal performance evaluations an example of [YOUR COMPANY NAME]'s commitment to our employees' career development and satisfaction. These [*Frequency of performance appraisals, i.e., "quarterly" or "yearly"*] assessments give us an opportunity to discuss goals, identify and correct weaknesses, acknowledge and encourage strengths, and formulate action plans. Your performance appraisal is scheduled for [*Date of performance appraisal*] beginning at [*Time the performance appraisal begins*] in [*Place within office where performance appraisal will be held*].

There is no reason for any apprehension over a performance appraisal. This scheduled review is truly an opportunity to focus on mutually beneficial actions and plans. I look forward to this chance to discuss in detail your career at [YOUR COMPANY NAME].

cc: [COPIES TO]

Approval

[DATE]

[Mr./Mrs./Ms./Dr.] [CUSTOMER'S FULL NAME]
[CUSTOMER'S TITLE]
[COMPANY]
[ADDRESS]
[CITY], [STATE] [ZIP CODE]

Dear [Mr./Mrs./Ms./Dr.] [CUSTOMER'S LAST NAME]:

Good habits encourage personal and professional growth. It is important to [YOUR COMPANY NAME] that our customers exhibit admirable business practices. We prefer to deal with companies whose rigorous operational standards match our own.

Thank you for allowing us to verify your credit history. After thoroughly reviewing [COMPANY]'s request, we are pleased to grant your organization credit terms and establish a monthly billing cycle.

[COMPANY]'s account credit limit is $[*Dollar amount of credit on* COMPANY's *account*] subject to the following terms and conditions: [*Describe all terms and conditions of credit extension*]. The individual responsible for expert handling of [COMPANY]'s account, [*First and last name of* YOUR COMPANY NAME's *credit representative*], should be available at all times to answer any questions. Speaking for our entire company, I thank you again for giving us the opportunity to serve [COMPANY]. We never compromise on our standards, and we look forward to a long business relationship.

Sincerely yours,

[YOUR NAME]
[YOUR TITLE]

Attendance and Punctuality

TO: [*First and last name of person receiving memo*]

FROM: [YOUR NAME]
[YOUR TITLE]

DATE: [DATE]

SUBJECT: Attendance and Punctuality Reminder

Let's be candid. Getting to work on time every day is probably not what most would consider fun. We'd rather be fishing, playing sports, reading, or maybe just loafing around in front of the television. We can't though; we have responsibilities to ourselves, our families, and our employers.

When fulfilling these obligations, we make commitments to be dependable and reliable in our actions. Others trust us to honor those commitments.

As your employer, [YOUR COMPANY NAME] expects you to arrive at work at the scheduled time. Absenteeism and tardiness are in direct conflict with the commitment you have made to us.

We don't take very well to people breaking their promises. It puts additional burdens on the company and your co-workers. In the rare instance when you will be late or unable to work as scheduled, advise [*First and last name of supervisor whom person receiving memo should contact regarding absenteeism or tardiness*] as soon as possible.

Let's be candid again. Continued disregard of your commitment to be on time every scheduled work day may result in disciplinary action, which may include termination of employment with [YOUR COMPANY NAME]. While you could have fun every day then, we think the drawbacks are obvious.

cc: [COPIES TO]

Attention Drawn to a Problem

TO: [*First and last name of person receiving memo*]

FROM: [YOUR NAME]
[YOUR TITLE]

DATE: [DATE]

SUBJECT: Thank You

There is a tendency to be overconfident when things are going well. We forget to pay attention to details or, worse, fail to give proper thought to our actions. The earlier the problem is recognized, the better.

Although this may sound strange, I want to thank you for voicing your concerns regarding my [*Describe the problem using first and last name of person receiving memo identified*]. You helped me recognize the immediate and long-term detrimental effects of this shortcoming.

Please know that I have made a commitment to follow your suggestions and change for my own and [YOUR COMPANY NAME]'s benefit. [*Name of person receiving memo identified*], again I extend my thanks for caring enough to make me aware of the problem before it had a chance to damage my career.

cc: [COPIES TO]

Auto Insurance Claim

[DATE]

[Mr./Mrs./Ms./Dr.] [FIRST AND LAST NAME]
[TITLE]
[COMPANY]
[ADDRESS]
[CITY], [STATE] [ZIP CODE]

Dear [Mr./Mrs./Ms./Dr.] [LAST NAME]:

There is never a good time for misfortune to occur. [YOUR COMPANY NAME] was recently reminded of this when one of our company vehicles was involved in an accident. After reviewing our [COMPANY] insurance policy, number [YOUR COMPANY NAME's *insurance policy number assigned by* COMPANY], this letter is sent in full compliance within the time limitations governing damage reimbursement.

The vehicle involved in the accident is car number [*Number of car described on* YOUR COMPANY NAME's *insurance policy number assigned by* COMPANY] on the policy. [*Describe vehicle with year, make, model and serial number as relates to Number of car described on* YOUR COMPANY NAME's *insurance policy number assigned by* COMPANY]. Reconstructing the accident in words alone is awkward. However, to the best of my knowledge, the driver, [*First and last name of driver involved in accident*], a [YOUR COMPANY NAME] employee, was [*Describe and list by number what happened before accident]*. Then, [*Describe and list by number how accident occurred*].

Damage estimates are attached for your reference. Please advise what effect, if any, this accident claim will have on our premiums and how we should proceed from here. Thank you for your assistance in securing reimbursement at the earliest date. I would like to move past this situation as quickly as possible.

Sincerely yours,

[YOUR NAME]
[YOUR TITLE]

Bad Attitude

TO: [*First and last name of person receiving memo*]

FROM: [YOUR NAME]
[YOUR TITLE]

DATE: [DATE]

SUBJECT: Apology

In reaching for the gold, challenging circumstances can bring out the darker side of people. We can become so focused on a single goal that we treat normal everyday tasks as annoying interruptions. Although the [*Describe the legitimate new task you have been assigned*] has been a welcome professional challenge, I recognize that it has caused changes in my normal demeanor.

Have confidence that my acknowledgment of this atypical behavior will have a positive effect. From this point forward, I promise to pay special attention to meeting the challenge with utmost enthusiasm. Thank you for understanding.

cc: [COPIES TO]

Bad Credit Card

[DATE]

[Mr./Mrs./Ms./Dr.] [CUSTOMER'S FULL NAME]
[CUSTOMER'S TITLE]
[COMPANY]
[ADDRESS]
[CITY], [STATE] [ZIP CODE]

Dear [Mr./Mrs./Ms./Dr.] [CUSTOMER'S LAST NAME]:

Does it ever seem to you that identification numbers control our world? We have driver's license, social security, telephone, and credit card numbers. Recently, [YOUR COMPANY NAME] tried to process [COMPANY]'s order for [*Name of product order*], and there was a slight problem with the credit card number you provided.

Because it's so easy to transpose numbers, please take a moment to confirm the following: Name on the Account: [*Name provided for* COMPANY's *credit card*] Issuer: [*Issuer of* COMPANY's *credit card*] Credit Card Number: [*Number provided for* COMPANY's *credit card*] Expiration Date: [*Expiration date provided for* COMPANY's *credit card*] If we have made an error or you would like us to charge another credit card, please telephone [*First and last name of person to call at* YOUR COMPANY NAME *with the telephone number*] at your earliest convenience. That's all it takes to speed [*Name of product order*] on its way to [COMPANY].

Thank you for helping us serve you.

Sincerely yours,

[YOUR NAME]
[YOUR TITLE]

Bad Goods Complaint

[DATE]

[Mr./Mrs./Ms./Dr.] [FIRST AND LAST NAME]
[TITLE]
[COMPANY]
[ADDRESS]
[CITY], [STATE] [ZIP CODE]

Dear [Mr./Mrs./Ms./Dr.] [LAST NAME]:

I want to say good-bye to our post-purchase blues. Being consumer-conscious, [YOUR COMPANY NAME] practices standard buying etiquette. Purchases are investigated and opinions gathered before our company authorizes spending.

Our experience with [*Name of bad product*] bought on [*Date name of bad product was purchased*] for $[*Dollar amount of name of bad product's purchase price*] does not match the product literature or testimonial claims. Specifically, [*Name of bad product*] falls dramatically short in the following manner: [*Describe and list by number problems with name of bad product*].

It is my hope that a refund will be expedited to protect our opinion of [COMPANY]. I have never believed the adage, "you get what you pay for." Money is an immaterial issue. Any product should, at the very minimum, leave a buyer satisfied with his or her purchase and the company that sold it. I look forward to the immediate refund that quells the "farewell"rising from my gullet.

Sincerely yours,

[YOUR NAME]
[YOUR TITLE]

Bad Service Complaint

[DATE]

[Mr./Mrs./Ms./Dr.] [FIRST AND LAST NAME]
[TITLE]
[COMPANY]
[ADDRESS]
[CITY], [STATE] [ZIP CODE]

Dear [Mr./Mrs./Ms./Dr.] [LAST NAME]:

Have you seen the advertisements or noticed a trend in titles on The *New York Times*, nonfiction best-seller list? Actually, you don't even need to pick up a book or magazine to see that service has become a thread that runs through the fabric of business the world over.

Today, the word "service" is thrown around as if it were something brand new. Service, however, has had the power to make or break sellers for as long as there have been buyers. I would like to help [COMPANY] by relating an incident exposing lack of respect and abominable service.

On [*Date of bad service*], [YOUR COMPANY NAME] had the unpleasant experience of [*Describe the incident*]. Not being a company to create waves, we handled the issue tactfully by [*Describe* YOUR COMPANY NAME's *reaction to Describe the incident*].

The average person is commonly believed to have at least 200 acquaintances. Bad news spreads like wildfire. I hope this type of experience is one your company calls the exception rather than the rule.

Sincerely yours,

[YOUR NAME]
[YOUR TITLE]

Bartering Agreement

[DATE]

[Mr./Mrs./Ms./Dr.] [FIRST AND LAST NAME]
[TITLE]
[COMPANY]
[ADDRESS]
[CITY], [STATE] [ZIP CODE]

Dear [Mr./Mrs./Ms./Dr.] [LAST NAME]:

Long before paper currency was invented in China around the 11th century, trade was the primary means of obtaining goods and services. Today, hundreds of years later, bartering is still an efficient and effective way of conducting business. Simply stated, you have something I need and I have something you desire.

Considering our respective business interests, I foresee an even exchange. To better our operations, [YOUR COMPANY NAME] has investigated various offerings for [*Name of product or service* YOUR COMPANY NAME *needs*] by companies like [COMPANY]. Your company is one of the leaders. Rather than paying cash for [*Specific name of product or service offered by* COMPANY, I propose a trade for [YOUR COMPANY NAME]'s [*Specific name of product or service offered by* YOUR COMPANY NAME].

Looking at the hard costs involved, value is well-covered without any currency exchange. [*First name of person receiving letter*], think about it and if this is not acceptable, perhaps you can suggest another way to achieve the same goal. The key is to strike a fair and equitable trade for the mutual benefit of the parties involved. I look forward to hearing from you in the near future.

Sincerely yours,

[YOUR NAME]
[YOUR TITLE]

Bend Company Policy Adjustment

[DATE]

[Mr./Mrs./Ms./Dr.] [CUSTOMER'S FULL NAME]
[CUSTOMER'S TITLE]
[COMPANY]
[ADDRESS]
[CITY], [STATE] [ZIP CODE]

Dear [Mr./Mrs./Ms./Dr.] [CUSTOMER'S LAST NAME]:

Policies govern companies and allow customers to buy with confidence. Policies cannot be so rigid, however, that they cause us to be unresponsive to the needs of a dynamic world.

[COMPANY]'s experience with [*Describe* COMPANY's *adjustment request*] is very unusual. Having recently become aware of the circumstances surrounding [*Describe* COMPANY's *adjustment request*], I understand your disappointment. There is no precedent worth invoking when our relationship with a customer is at stake.

You have [YOUR COMPANY NAME]'s promise that we will [*Describe actions taken by* YOUR COMPANY NAME *to do* COMPANY's *adjustment request*]. In the face of life's uncertainties, there remains something [COMPANY] can rely on. Day after day, [YOUR COMPANY NAME] dedicates itself to customer satisfaction. Thank you for allowing [YOUR COMPANY NAME] to participate in [COMPANY]'s future.

Sincerely yours,

[YOUR NAME]
[YOUR TITLE]

Best and Final Quote

[DATE]

[Mr./Mrs./Ms./Dr.] [CUSTOMER'S FULL NAME]
[CUSTOMER'S TITLE]
[COMPANY]
[ADDRESS]
[CITY], [STATE] [ZIP CODE]

Dear [Mr./Mrs./Ms./Dr.] [CUSTOMER'S LAST NAME]:

Isn't it better to spend a little more now than a lot more later? Experienced business professionals like you appreciate the value of responsiveness and customer satisfaction. Too many executives tell horror stories about problems caused by vendors who neglected them after the sale.

Supplier qualifications and price structures are both important buying criteria. Although [YOUR COMPANY NAME]'s response to bid number [*Provide* COMPANY's *bid tracking number*], for [*Describe what the bid was for*], was quite competitive, additional discount solicitations from customers are given priority. [COMPANY]'s request for [YOUR COMPANY NAME]'s best and final offer demanded top management intervention.

The final pricing structure review pinpointed areas in which discounts could be delivered without compromising our standards. These are as follows: [*Describe the price reduction*].

In selecting [YOUR COMPANY NAME]'s proposal, [COMPANY] is assured of both a fair price and our pledge to provide immediate and long-term operational advantages. Other companies try to imitate us; none even compares. Give us a chance, and you will join the other [YOUR COMPANY NAME] customers who loudly proclaim, "They give the best product value, quality, and service while keeping costs quite competitive."

Sincerely yours,

[YOUR NAME]
[YOUR TITLE]

Bid Acceptance

[DATE]

[Mr./Mrs./Ms./Dr.] [FIRST AND LAST NAME]
[TITLE]
[COMPANY]
[ADDRESS]
[CITY], [STATE] [ZIP CODE]

Dear [Mr./Mrs./Ms./Dr.] [LAST NAME]:

Effort combined with knowledge and tenacity is the springboard of accomplishment. One feat alone does not result in success; an ongoing pattern unfolds every time a customer is encountered. [COMPANY]'s response to our specifications demonstrated, more than any other response we received, a thorough understanding of [YOUR COMPANY NAME]'s needs.

Therefore, this letter serves as formal notification that [YOUR COMPANY NAME] awards the contract for [*Describe what the bid was for*], identified by [YOUR COMPANY NAME]'s bid number [*Provide the bid tracking number relating to what the bid was for*], to [COMPANY]. We should meet within the upcoming week to review an action plan that will take us from start to finish as outlined in the proposal. As [COMPANY]'s professionalism won our business, know that your adherence to commitments made by [COMPANY] during the bidding process is paramount.

The way in which this project is handled may result in additional business opportunities for [COMPANY]. With that said and understood, congratulations on positioning your company with [YOUR COMPANY NAME]. Obviously, you spent many hours in and out of our offices preparing the successful proposal. I look forward to getting started on "our" project.

Sincerely yours,

[YOUR NAME]
[YOUR TITLE]

Bid Announcement

[DATE]

[Mr./Mrs./Ms./Dr.] [FIRST AND LAST NAME]
[TITLE]
[COMPANY]
[ADDRESS]
[CITY], [STATE] [ZIP CODE]

Dear [Mr./Mrs./Ms./Dr.] [LAST NAME]:

In any contest, there can be only one winner. [YOUR COMPANY NAME] challenges [COMPANY] to provide the most competitive bid and detailed proposal for [*Describe what the bid is for*]. Budgetary funds are allocated for [*Describe what the bid is for*], [YOUR COMPANY NAME] bid number [*Provide* YOUR COMPANY NAME's *bid tracking number relating to what the bid is for*]; our anticipated procurement date is [*Date what the bid is for will be procured*].

[COMPANY]'s proposal should include specific details organized by chapter number in the following manner:

1. [COMPANY] Introduction and Background
2. [*Describe what the bid is for*] Features and Warranty Information
3. [COMPANY] References
4. [*Describe what the bid is for*] Pricing
5. [*Describe what the bid is for*] Documentation and Literature

[YOUR COMPANY NAME] is holding a bidders' conference to address specific requirements and evaluation criteria on [*Date of bidders' conference*] at [*Location of bidders' conference*] beginning at [*Time bidders' conference begins*]. To ensure equality among the respondents, no questions pertaining to the bid will be answered before the conference. I look forward to seeing you there.

Sincerely yours,

[YOUR NAME]
[YOUR TITLE]

Bid Best Price Request

[DATE]

[Mr./Mrs./Ms./Dr.] [FIRST AND LAST NAME]
[TITLE]
[COMPANY]
[ADDRESS]
[CITY], [STATE] [ZIP CODE]

Dear [Mr./Mrs./Ms./Dr.] [LAST NAME]:

The results are in. Congratulations on [COMPANY]'s selection as a finalist for [YOUR COMPANY NAME]'s competitive bid number [*Provide* YOUR COMPANY NAME's *bid tracking number relating to what the bid is for*] for [*Describe what the bid is for*]. The proposal submitted clearly reflects [COMPANY]'s market and product awareness.

However, the decision committee requires your assistance once more before determining the winner. Respondent bids are quite similar. We are giving finalists the opportunity to submit their best and final pricing offers for [*Describe what the bid is for*] under the bid's existing conditions, quantity, and terms.

While a pricing revision is not required to remain a finalist, a response either way must be in our office by the close of business on [*Date response is due*]. Be advised that all finalists have received this letter, and obviously, it is in [COMPANY]'s best interest to revisit the pricing. On behalf of [YOUR COMPANY NAME], thank you for your continued professionalism. We look forward to receiving what could be the winning bid.

Sincerely yours,

[YOUR NAME]
[YOUR TITLE]

Bid Rejection

[DATE]

[Mr./Mrs./Ms./Dr.] [FIRST AND LAST NAME]
[TITLE]
[COMPANY]
[ADDRESS]
[CITY], [STATE] [ZIP CODE]

Dear [Mr./Mrs./Ms./Dr.] [LAST NAME]:

Competition is beneficial to both buyers and sellers. During a bidding process, customer demands test vendor operations. The customer then chooses the one company best suited to be its partner for the next project.

It was evident that you and [COMPANY] expended much time and effort in completing [YOUR COMPANY NAME]'s bid for [*Describe what the bid was for*]. I know well how costly and time-intensive a bid of this nature is to complete accurately and thoroughly. Please be advised, however, that the decision committee did not select [COMPANY] as the winner.

Although [COMPANY] was not awarded this bid, I hope to see your company name in future competitive situations. It may be possible for us to join forces under different conditions. [*First name of person receiving letter*], thank you for your response. I assure you that our decision is not a reflection on your expertise or professionalism.

Sincerely yours,

[YOUR NAME]
[YOUR TITLE]

Bid Revision

[DATE]

[Mr./Mrs./Ms./Dr.] [FIRST AND LAST NAME]
[TITLE]
[COMPANY]
[ADDRESS]
[CITY], [STATE] [ZIP CODE]

Dear [Mr./Mrs./Ms./Dr.] [LAST NAME]:

As additional information is gathered, decisions are subject to change. Many respondents to [YOUR COMPANY NAME]'s bid, number [*Provide* YOUR COMPANY NAME's *bid tracking number relating to what the bid is for*], for [*Describe what the bid is for*], have requested [*Describe and list by number bid respondent's request*]. The decision committee considered the issue and decided to [*Describe and list by number the revision*].

Therefore, please revise [COMPANY]'s bid response to incorporate the aforementioned. Any questions pertaining to this modification must be submitted in writing to promote fairness among the respondents.

Upon our receipt of a question, we will promptly provide the question and answer to all bid participants. Thank you for your assistance in ensuring that [YOUR COMPANY NAME] ethics are maintained during the bid process. It's important for both of us.

Sincerely yours,

[YOUR NAME]
[YOUR TITLE]

Billing Adjustment

[DATE]

[Mr./Mrs./Ms./Dr.] [FIRST AND LAST NAME]
[TITLE]
[COMPANY]
[ADDRESS]
[CITY], [STATE] [ZIP CODE]

Dear [Mr./Mrs./Ms./Dr.] [LAST NAME]:

There is no doubt about it; mistakes happen. In today's computer age, information management is supposedly above reproach. [YOUR COMPANY NAME] understands that just one incorrect keystroke can add the wrong column of figures or erase an entire file of customer requests. It appears that this was the case on invoice number [*Number generated by* COMPANY *on the invoice*] recently sent by [COMPANY].

Upon checking our records authorizing the purchase of [*Describe and list by number* YOUR COMPANY NAME's *purchases within number generated by* COMPANY *on the invoice*], we have discovered that [*Place where there is an error in number generated by* COMPANY *on the invoice*] contains an error. The correct [*Place where there is an error in the number generated by* COMPANY *on the invoice*] should be [*Describe the correction needed*]. I am confident that [COMPANY]'s due diligence will result in the same correction arrived at by our staff.

Over the years, I have learned computers are merely machines and only as good as the humans and programs that control them. We are prone to error, and so are the machines. Thank you for your prompt attention in this matter and your help in making the necessary billing adjustments. It takes one more pressure off my day.

Sincerely yours,

[YOUR NAME]
[YOUR TITLE]

Billing Error Apology

[DATE]

[Mr./Mrs./Ms./Dr.] [CUSTOMER'S FULL NAME]
[CUSTOMER'S TITLE]
[COMPANY]
[ADDRESS]
[CITY], [STATE] [ZIP CODE]

Dear [Mr./Mrs./Ms./Dr.] [CUSTOMER'S LAST NAME]:

A prosperity-bound company modifies operations the moment it recognizes an area of weakness. [YOUR COMPANY NAME] appreciates [COMPANY]'s diligence in pointing out an error in your billing statement. I am embarrassed by this failure of our accounting controls and have taken immediate steps to prevent similar errors in the future.

We have rectified the situation with actions rather than words. The statement was corrected to reflect [*Describe how statement was corrected*]. Please accept my apologies for any inconvenience we may have caused. [YOUR COMPANY NAME] believes that customers are the ultimate directors of our future. Thank you for taking the time to give us some guidance.

Sincerely yours,

[YOUR NAME]
[YOUR TITLE]

Bounced Check

[DATE]

[Mr./Mrs./Ms./Dr.] [CUSTOMER'S FULL NAME]
[CUSTOMER'S TITLE]
[COMPANY]
[ADDRESS]
[CITY], [STATE] [ZIP CODE]

Dear [Mr./Mrs./Ms./Dr.] [CUSTOMER'S LAST NAME]:

Textbook budgeting theories are difficult to implement in business. Especially in a growth company like [COMPANY], emergency expenditures can create havoc in money management. Although I am not positive, I suspect that this may be happening at your company.

The [COMPANY] check [YOUR COMPANY NAME] received as payment for [*Describe what the check was for*] was returned to us by the bank on [*Date* YOUR COMPANY NAME *received check back*] because of insufficient funds. For your records, the draft posing the problem is check number [*Number on* COMPANY's *check*], in the amount of $[*Amount of* COMPANY's *check*], written on [*Date the check was written*].

Based on [COMPANY]'s previous professional practices, I assume that maintaining an honorable reputation is just as important to you as it is to us. We want to put this embarrassing situation behind us and move forward in our business relationship. Before this can happen, however, [YOUR COMPANY NAME] must have $[*Amount of* COMPANY's *check*] by [*Date* COMPANY *must resubmit payment to* YOUR COMPANY NAME]. Thank you, and please remember that if there are extenuating circumstances, we will work with you.

Sincerely yours,

[YOUR NAME]
[YOUR TITLE]

Business Association Inquiry

[DATE]

[Mr./Mrs./Ms./Dr.] [FIRST AND LAST NAME]
[TITLE]
[COMPANY]
[ADDRESS]
[CITY], [STATE] [ZIP CODE]

Dear [Mr./Mrs./Ms./Dr.] [LAST NAME]:

It's good to have strong partners. In personal and professional relationships, I strive for a sharing of beliefs, goals, interests, and values. Joining forces with like-minded people can have a decidedly positive effect on our lives.

Believing we may have complementary aspirations, I am interested in [COMPANY]. Please send an introductory membership package to my attention at [YOUR COMPANY NAME *address*]. Specifically, I would like to review the dues, meeting schedule, typical member profile, and any educational seminars sponsored by the group.

Thank you for your reply to my inquiry about what may prove a mutually beneficial relationship. Networking with other professionals has proven repeatedly to be both a learning and a rewarding experience.

Sincerely yours,

[YOUR NAME]
[YOUR TITLE]

Business Competition

TO: [*First and last name of person receiving memo*]

FROM: [YOUR NAME]
[YOUR TITLE]

DATE: [DATE]

SUBJECT: Competition Update

Competition in business sparks progress. Knowing that another organization is pursuing the same goal makes us work harder and smarter. Having [*Name of competitor*] in our industry, therefore, is not a bad thing.

Their market placement reveals an unstable foundation that is working to our advantage. The key is to expose these facts to our customers in an ethical and professional manner. We never want to appear to be "bad-mouthing" the competition.

Making negative comments about competitors inevitably lowers our credibility. When asked about [*Name of competitor*], keep comments brief and vague while communicating your confidence that our [*Name of your product or service*] is of the finest quality. We have a long-standing reputation and a list of satisfied customers behind us.

Our persistence in maintaining standards for excellence will beat the competition. They are not the last challenge we face, only the most recent. Take [*Name of competitor*]'s very mention as an invitation to advance professionally by focusing a little more on success.

cc: [COPIES TO]

Business Expansion

[DATE]

[Mr./Mrs./Ms./Dr.] [CUSTOMER'S FULL NAME]
[CUSTOMER'S TITLE]
[COMPANY]
[ADDRESS]
[CITY], [STATE] [ZIP CODE]

Dear [Mr./Mrs./Ms./Dr.] [CUSTOMER'S LAST NAME]:

Like a child, a business begins to mature the moment those first baby steps are taken. Lessons are learned, directions become focused, and in time, strength coupled with determination makes a marathon runner. For both individuals and enterprises, the road to adulthood is simultaneously rocky and rewarding.

Congratulations on paving a prosperous path for your company, your employees, and their families. As your expansion demonstrates, [COMPANY] has developed the attributes that help companies win awards. I extend my wishes for your continued success, and when time allows, I would like to discuss how [YOUR COMPANY NAME] might be of assistance in [COMPANY]'s explosive growth.

Sincerely yours,

[YOUR NAME]
[YOUR TITLE]

Buy Extended Warranty

[DATE]

[Mr./Mrs./Ms./Dr.] [CUSTOMER'S FULL NAME]
[CUSTOMER'S TITLE]
[COMPANY]
[ADDRESS]
[CITY], [STATE] [ZIP CODE]

Dear [Mr./Mrs./Ms./Dr.] [CUSTOMER'S LAST NAME]:

Budget consciousness has prompted many companies to make cosmetic changes. Approaching business in this trendy way rarely affects bottom-line performance in the long term. A penny saved here today could cost a dollar there tomorrow.

We want to help [COMPANY] protect the significant investment made when it purchased [*Name of product*]. Certainly, [COMPANY] is planning to benefit from [*Name of product*] for more than the [*Length of existing warranty*] covered by the warranty. Therefore, we recommend an extended warranty agreement that lengthens the standard warranty period by [*Length of extended warranty*].

An extended warranty protects [COMPANY]'s investment. I will phone to set a time to discuss this additional customer-oriented opportunity with you. It is a budgetary line item well worth its cost. Let me present real dollar examples that make sense.

Sincerely yours,

[YOUR NAME]
[YOUR TITLE]

Cancel Order

[DATE]

[Mr./Mrs./Ms./Dr.] [FIRST AND LAST NAME]
[TITLE]
[COMPANY]
[ADDRESS]
[CITY], [STATE] [ZIP CODE]

Dear [Mr./Mrs./Ms./Dr.] [LAST NAME]:

We can control only the next few seconds of our lives. After that, so many variables come into play that even the most formidable plans are subject to change. On [*Date order was made*], [YOUR COMPANY NAME] placed an order for [*Describe and list by number what the order contained*] based upon information available at the time.

Unfortunately, new information makes it necessary for us to cancel the order immediately. The details surrounding cancellation are confidential. I have personally checked your cancellation policies and confirmed that we are in compliance with them.

Believe me, if I were at liberty to provide a full explanation, I would. Thank you for processing this cancellation promptly to obviate any additional work for either of our companies. This action is under [COMPANY]'s complete control.

Sincerely yours,

[YOUR NAME]
[YOUR TITLE]

Cancellation of Meeting

[DATE]

[Mr./Mrs./Ms./Dr.] [CUSTOMER'S FULL NAME]
[CUSTOMER'S TITLE]
[COMPANY]
[ADDRESS]
[CITY], [STATE] [ZIP CODE]

Dear [Mr./Mrs./Ms./Dr.] [CUSTOMER'S LAST NAME]:

Time is a precious commodity. Every tick of the clock marks another moment spent either fruitfully or frivolously. Considering how valuable your time is, I plan not to waste any of it.

It would be in your best interest if we waited until the appropriate resources were available for our meeting regarding [*Topic of meeting*]. The information we will discuss is still being gathered, and I do not want to present you with half the story. Therefore, I find it necessary to postpone the meeting scheduled on [*Date of meeting*] at [*Time of meeting*].

Given an additional [*Amount of time needed before meeting occurs*], we can give [COMPANY] all the attention it deserves. I apologize for any inconvenience and hope that this notice is sufficient to allow you to reschedule the time. Thank you for understanding. I want our time together to be spent wisely.

Sincerely yours,

[YOUR NAME]
[YOUR TITLE]

Cancellation of Credit by Grantor

[DATE]

[Mr./Mrs./Ms./Dr.] [CUSTOMER'S FULL NAME]
[CUSTOMER'S TITLE]
[COMPANY]
[ADDRESS]
[CITY], [STATE] [ZIP CODE]

Dear [Mr./Mrs./Ms./Dr.] [CUSTOMER'S LAST NAME]:

Extending credit is a demonstration of good faith. A business exchanges goods and services for promises of payment. When a debt goes unpaid, both the business and the customer suffer a loss.

Customers forfeit the convenience credit offers by not upholding their commitments. [YOUR COMPANY NAME]'s records indicate that [COMPANY]'s account is overdue by [*Length of time payment is overdue*] on an outstanding balance of $[*Dollar amount of* COMPANY's *overdue balance*]. At this point, it is in our mutual best interest to cancel your credit effective [*Date* COMPANY's *credit will be canceled*].

Not that this is the case with [COMPANY], but credit has led companies and people into financial trouble. We cannot extend ourselves or [COMPANY]'s credit line any further. If you believe our calculations are in error or there are mitigating circumstances delaying your payment, contact me immediately.

Please know that this is not my decision; I am merely the enforcer of the company policies that keep our operation running smoothly. I want to help [COMPANY] get back in our good graces in any way possible. Let's talk about how we can work toward this goal. I hope to hear from you soon.

Sincerely yours,

[YOUR NAME]
[YOUR TITLE]

Cancellation of Credit by Grantee

[DATE]

[Mr./Mrs./Ms./Dr.] [FIRST AND LAST NAME]
[TITLE]
[COMPANY]
[ADDRESS]
[CITY], [STATE] [ZIP CODE]

Dear [Mr./Mrs./Ms./Dr.] [LAST NAME]:

When great ideas have outlived their usefulness, it's time for a change. [YOUR COMPANY NAME]'s shift in direction has resulted in more than a few displacements as strategies have matured. Credit with [COMPANY] is one thing we no longer require for our long-term goal attainment.

Circumstances being what they are, I write on behalf of [YOUR COMPANY NAME] to cancel our [COMPANY] credit account, number [YOUR COMPANY NAME's *credit account number assigned by* COMPANY]. This is effective on [*Date the credit will be canceled*].

Please calculate the final balance as of the above date. To prevent any potential miscommunication, advise me of the total amount due in writing on [COMPANY] letterhead by [*Date the* COMPANY *should advise* YOUR COMPANY NAME *how much you owe*]. I appreciate your prompt attention and extend thanks for your participation in our growth.

Sincerely yours,

[YOUR NAME]
[YOUR TITLE]

Casual Reminder

[DATE]

[Mr./Mrs./Ms./Dr.] [CUSTOMER'S FULL NAME]
[CUSTOMER'S TITLE]
[COMPANY]
[ADDRESS]
[CITY], [STATE] [ZIP CODE]

Dear [Mr./Mrs./Ms./Dr.] [CUSTOMER'S LAST NAME]:

Life can be so hectic at times that even our habits fall by the wayside. We neglect the simple things like eating lunch or reading the paper. Many times, people call with requests, and we must drop everything to meet their expectations.

[COMPANY] has an obligation to [YOUR COMPANY NAME] too. Your credit history suggests that simple neglect is the reason for your lack of promptness in remitting payment to [YOUR COMPANY NAME]. Our records indicate that the amount of $[*Dollar amount of payment needed from* COMPANY] is currently past due by [*Length of time which dollar amount of payment needed from* COMPANY *is past due*].

It is never too late to make payment on the account. If this letter crossed paths with your check, please accept my apologies for this friendly reminder. We simply want to revive [COMPANY]'s good habits before the situation has a chance to get out of control. Thank you for your assistance.

Sincerely yours,

[YOUR NAME]
[YOUR TITLE]

Change in Business Hours

[DATE]

[Mr./Mrs./Ms./Dr.] [CUSTOMER'S FULL NAME]
[CUSTOMER'S TITLE]
[COMPANY]
[ADDRESS]
[CITY], [STATE] [ZIP CODE]

Dear [Mr./Mrs./Ms./Dr.] [CUSTOMER'S LAST NAME]:

Is there ever enough time in a day? [YOUR COMPANY NAME] is relentless in our quest to outperform the competition. Therefore, we've extended our hours to accommodate almost everyone's schedule.

[YOUR COMPANY NAME]'s offices are now ready to serve you from [*Time* YOUR COMPANY NAME's *offices open*] to [*Time* YOUR COMPANY NAME's *offices close*]. As always, you'll find our professional staff ready to help at all times.

This change in hours resulted from customer recommendations. If you have other suggestions, please let us know. We're known as the people's choice for a good reason. Simply stated, [YOUR COMPANY NAME]'s business is helping [COMPANY]'s business.

Sincerely yours,

[YOUR NAME]
[YOUR TITLE]

Change of Address

[DATE]

[Mr./Mrs./Ms./Dr.] [CUSTOMER'S FULL NAME]
[CUSTOMER'S TITLE]
[COMPANY]
[ADDRESS]
[CITY], [STATE] [ZIP CODE]

Dear [Mr./Mrs./Ms./Dr.] [CUSTOMER'S LAST NAME]:

Looking around our old offices, we see that we underestimated the effort required to move to a location from which we could better serve our customers. The time was well spent. Now [YOUR COMPANY NAME]'s friendly staff is improving on the superior service standards our customers have come to expect over the years.

Whether you keep important contacts in a card file, on a computer, in a pocket organizer, or on scraps of paper in your desk drawer, please be sure [YOUR COMPANY NAME]'s is correct.

Our new address and telephone number are:

Address: [YOUR COMPANY NAME's street address]
City, State, Zip Code: [YOUR COMPANY NAME's city, state, and zip code]
Telephone Number: [YOUR COMPANY NAME's telephone number]
Facsimile Number: [YOUR COMPANY NAME's facsimile number]

As always, we appreciate [COMPANY]'s business, and if you're ever in the area, do stop by. I don't know whether it's the extra space or just the increased enthusiasm, but I think the coffee is better here too!

Sincerely yours,

[YOUR NAME]
[YOUR TITLE]

Changes Approved

[DATE]

[Mr./Mrs./Ms./Dr.] [CUSTOMER'S FULL NAME]
[CUSTOMER'S TITLE]
[COMPANY]
[ADDRESS]
[CITY], [STATE] [ZIP CODE]

Dear [Mr./Mrs./Ms./Dr.] [CUSTOMER'S LAST NAME]:

Contracts serve as confirmation that verbal commitments will be honored throughout a business relationship. [YOUR COMPANY NAME] wants every agreement made with our customers to be a positive experience. We want you to sign with enthusiasm and without reservation.

Therefore, [COMPANY]'s request to modify [*Describe the changes approved*] on our contract for [*Describe what the contract is for*] is approved. Enclosed are the revised contracts for your review and signature. Please let me know the quickest way to obtain the executed agreements so [YOUR COMPANY NAME] can get started as soon as possible. Thank you for your assistance and confidence. I guarantee [COMPANY]'s complete satisfaction as we fulfill our commitments.

Sincerely yours,

[YOUR NAME]
[YOUR TITLE]

Check Not Signed

[DATE]

[Mr./Mrs./Ms./Dr.] [CUSTOMER'S FULL NAME]
[CUSTOMER'S TITLE]
[COMPANY]
[ADDRESS]
[CITY], [STATE] [ZIP CODE]

Dear [Mr./Mrs./Ms./Dr.] [CUSTOMER'S LAST NAME]:

Several prominent psychologists contend that our signatures reveal things about our personalities. Fine-tuned letters reflect a precise character; extending lines mark an extrovert. Unfortunately, even if we wanted to, we would be unable to analyze your personality on the check sent as payment for [*Describe the check's purpose*].

The check was received without the required signature. Therefore, [YOUR COMPANY NAME] is sending the check back to you. We expect a replacement, properly completed and signed, within the next [*Date by which* COMPANY *must resubmit check to* YOUR COMPANY NAME] business days. [YOUR COMPANY NAME] assumes this was an oversight rather than a reflection of [COMPANY]'s true character. Thank you for your prompt attention in this matter.

Sincerely yours,

[YOUR NAME]
[YOUR TITLE]

Colleague Review Transmittal

[DATE]

[Mr./Mrs./Ms./Dr.] [FIRST AND LAST NAME]
[TITLE]
[COMPANY]
[ADDRESS]
[CITY], [STATE] [ZIP CODE]

Dear [Mr./Mrs./Ms./Dr.] [LAST NAME]:

Experience is often gained in the pursuit of something else. Seasoned professionals know that lessons must be remembered and applied to be of use. Respecting you as I do, I hope to limit any harm to [YOUR COMPANY NAME] by offering the following for your feedback.

Briefly, our company is contemplating a move that appears worthy of a complete investigation. Your impressions would help us decide whether to pursue this further. Our particular interest lies in [*Describe your interest in project*].

I realize that your own projects take priority, and I appreciate your effort. Be assured that your constructive criticism will weigh heavily in our analysis. I look forward to hearing your professional opinion. [*First name of person receiving letter*], thank you.

Sincerely yours,

[YOUR NAME]
[YOUR TITLE]

Community Work

[DATE]

[Mr./Mrs./Ms./Dr.] [CUSTOMER'S FULL NAME]
[CUSTOMER'S TITLE]
[COMPANY]
[ADDRESS]
[CITY], [STATE] [ZIP CODE]

Dear [Mr./Mrs./Ms./Dr.] [CUSTOMER'S LAST NAME]:

Business stresses and successes harden many people to the problems of the less fortunate. I, for example, used to view the homeless with disgust, thinking, "They could get jobs." Then I came to realize that something had happened in their lives that made them give up on their dreams.

We all have ambitions; some are simply more grandiose than others. In moving toward our goals, challenges either make us stronger or weaken the pursuit. Because we have not relinquished our dreams, it is our responsibility to help those who may have given up.

I respect you for understanding the benefits of helping the underprivileged. Your compassionate efforts to [*Describe the community program's goal*] are commendable. No doubt, the time you have spent has had far-reaching effects on their lives. Please let me know if I can help with the program in any way. It would be my pleasure.

Sincerely yours,

[YOUR NAME]
[YOUR TITLE]

Company Received Award

TO: All Staff

FROM: [YOUR NAME]
[YOUR TITLE]

DATE: [DATE]

SUBJECT: Reputation for Excellence Confirmed as [YOUR COMPANY NAME] Receives Award

Think of the last time you watched a sports event, perhaps a baseball or football game. Dig a bit deeper into your memory, and you can't help noticing a few characteristics exhibited by the winning team. I'm talking about the team's coordination, determination, and commitment to excellence.

Even though a single player threw the winning pass or hit a home run, that one play alone didn't make the game a success. Every team member played an integral role and brought a different talent to the field, enabling all to reach the ultimate goal. Because of your individual contributions to our company and our team, [YOUR COMPANY NAME] was recognized by [*Name of organization that gave award*] for [*Describe the reason for award*] and received their prestigious [*Name of award*] award.

Thank you for your winning attitude every game, every day. With your support, we can do it again!

cc: [COPIES TO]

Company Sponsored Event

[DATE]

[Mr./Mrs./Ms./Dr.] [CUSTOMER'S FULL NAME]
[CUSTOMER'S TITLE]
[COMPANY]
[ADDRESS]
[CITY], [STATE] [ZIP CODE]

Dear [Mr./Mrs./Ms./Dr.] [CUSTOMER'S LAST NAME]:

Isn't it time you took a break? While listening to the radio or reading the paper, you may have become aware of an exciting event coming to town. In getting the news out about [*Name of event*], the media occasionally neglect to mention the sponsors making this calendar item possible.

[YOUR COMPANY NAME] is proud to be a corporate sponsor of [*Name of event*] on [*Date of event*] at [*Specific location of event*]. We invite you to be our special guest at this event, and it is my honor to arrange your guest passes. Knowing how hard you work, I suspect that this will be a welcome break in your daily routine. Just reach for your telephone and tell me you'll be there, and it'll be a done deal.

Sincerely yours,

[YOUR NAME]
[YOUR TITLE]

Competition

[DATE]

[Mr./Mrs./Ms./Dr.] [CUSTOMER'S FULL NAME]
[CUSTOMER'S TITLE]
[COMPANY]
[ADDRESS]
[CITY], [STATE] [ZIP CODE]

Dear [Mr./Mrs./Ms./Dr.] [CUSTOMER'S LAST NAME]:

Throughout the world, budding artists study technique in the towns where renowned masters lived and worked. However, some of today's students are doing much more than painting. They are creating Monets, da Vincis, Picassos, and Van Goghs in a fraction of the time it took the artists to create the originals.

By studying brushstrokes with a magnifying glass, today's artists can produce reproductions that create havoc in the art market. Aging techniques are applied to further increase the apparent authenticity of the counterfeits. The results are copies even the experts have trouble identifying.

[YOUR COMPANY NAME] is the leader in [*Describe* YOUR COMPANY NAME's *main business emphasis and what you are trying to market to* COMPANY *that has competition*]; we regularly receive awards for our continuing excellence. Our best honors do not adorn our office walls, however; they are our repeat customers.

Don't be swayed by second-rate reproductions. If you have any questions about our works, I would be happy to show you some critical reviews and provide a magnifying glass with which you can make your own examination. No other company even comes close to [YOUR COMPANY NAME]. We're number one now and will remain so for many years to come.

Sincerely yours,

[YOUR NAME]
[YOUR TITLE]

Computer Error Apology

[DATE]

[Mr./Mrs./Ms./Dr.] [CUSTOMER'S FULL NAME]
[CUSTOMER'S TITLE]
[COMPANY]
[ADDRESS]
[CITY], [STATE] [ZIP CODE]

Dear [Mr./Mrs./Ms./Dr.] [CUSTOMER'S LAST NAME]:

Imagine a world without computer technology. From ordinary appliances to sophisticated satellite systems, computers are everywhere. As business relies on technology for more and more of its everyday operations, we begin to presume that the machines are infallible.

Recently, [YOUR COMPANY NAME] was reminded that this presumption can be dangerous. You may have noticed this on [*Describe how* COMPANY *was affected by computer error*]. Although the problem was corrected immediately, my concern is [COMPANY]'s impression of [YOUR COMPANY NAME].

Our expert staff has spent many hours working to eliminate the possibility of any future system mishaps. I appreciate your understanding. We've pledged to work harder than ever.

Sincerely yours,

[YOUR NAME]
[YOUR TITLE]

Confirm Equipment Rental

[DATE]

[Mr./Mrs./Ms./Dr.] [FIRST AND LAST NAME]
[TITLE]
[COMPANY]
[ADDRESS]
[CITY], [STATE] [ZIP CODE]

Dear [Mr./Mrs./Ms./Dr.] [LAST NAME]:

Proper tools make our businesses run smoothly. In the perfect business world, every company would have the right equipment for every job it might have to undertake. However, this would eliminate the need for companies like [COMPANY] and, as your apparent success demonstrates, is not realistic.

[YOUR COMPANY NAME] runs a tight ship. When our goal attainment is dependent on another company's actions, our policy is to confirm those arrangements.

I trust the [*Describe and list by number equipment rented*] will be delivered to [*Address to which equipment rented will be delivered*] on [*Date equipment rented will be delivered*] around [*Time equipment rented will be delivered*] as we have agreed. Please take a moment today to verify the above details and advise me that everything is in order. Thank you for your continuing assistance and commitment to professional service. [COMPANY] is one of the tools of our trade.

Sincerely,

[YOUR NAME]
[YOUR TITLE]

Confirm Event Attendance

[DATE]

[Mr./Mrs./Ms./Dr.] [FIRST AND LAST NAME]
[TITLE]
[COMPANY]
[ADDRESS]
[CITY], [STATE] [ZIP CODE]

Dear [Mr./Mrs./Ms./Dr.] [LAST NAME]:

Can we ever be too efficient in business? [YOUR COMPANY NAME] doesn't think so. A little checking now eliminates errors later.

We usually receive an acknowledgment of some type when reservations are made for an event such as [*Name of event*]. Since we have not, I take this opportunity to confirm our reservation for [*Name of event*] on [*Date of event*] beginning at [*Time event starts*].

The reservation is in the name(s) of [*First and last name(s) of persons holding the reservation*]. Unless we hear otherwise, we'll assume all systems are go and we are free to allow our anticipation to grow as the date nears. See you there!

Sincerely yours,

[YOUR NAME]
[YOUR TITLE]

Confirm Phone Conversation

[DATE]

[Mr./Mrs./Ms./Dr.] [FIRST AND LAST NAME]
[TITLE]
[COMPANY]
[ADDRESS]
[CITY], [STATE] [ZIP CODE]

Dear [Mr./Mrs./Ms./Dr.] [LAST NAME]:

By most estimates, there are between 3,000 and 4,000 languages in the world. Mandarin has the largest number of speakers; English the second. Although we speak the same language in more ways than one, miscommunication can sour any undertaking.

To confirm that our business dialects are complementary, a quick synopsis of our telephone conversation on [*Date telephone conversation took place*] is in order. It is my understanding that [YOUR COMPANY NAME] is to [*Describe and list by number future actions by* YOUR COMPANY NAME]. [COMPANY] is planning to [*Describe and list by number future actions by* COMPANY].

If I am interpreting any area incorrectly, please advise me at your earliest convenience. Thank you for your professionalism now and in the future. While some languages have millions of speakers and others only 25, I am pleased ours is shared.

Sincerely yours,

[YOUR NAME]
[YOUR TITLE]

Confirm Reservations

[DATE]

[Mr./Mrs./Ms./Dr.] [FIRST AND LAST NAME]
[TITLE]
[COMPANY]
[ADDRESS]
[CITY], [STATE] [ZIP CODE]

Dear [Mr./Mrs./Ms./Dr.] [LAST NAME]:

Every day, millions of reservations are processed for everything from champagne balloon rides at sunrise to safaris crossing the African veldt. While I wish our reservations for [*Describe what reservation is for*] were for one of the above adventures, the conventional importance of details must be addressed.

Therefore, I am confirming our reservation for [*Describe what reservation is for*] on [*Date of reservation*]. [COMPANY] will be [*Describe and list by number actions need by* COMPANY *concerning what reservation is for*]. Please take a moment to verify the above and advise me of any potential problem areas. Thank you for your assistance; who knows, maybe we'll experience eccentricity more than once in our lives. I hear African safaris are a natural wonder.

Sincerely yours,

[YOUR NAME]
[YOUR TITLE]

Confirmation of Business Meeting

[DATE]

[Mr./Mrs./Ms./Dr.] [CUSTOMER'S FULL NAME]
[CUSTOMER'S TITLE]
[COMPANY]
[ADDRESS]
[CITY], [STATE] [ZIP CODE]

Dear [Mr./Mrs./Ms./Dr.] [CUSTOMER'S LAST NAME]:

Professionals can spend as much as half of every day in meetings. Sometimes it feels as if we live in the conference room. And, that doesn't count the time we spend preparing for those meetings.

I have worked hard to ensure that our meeting on [*Date of meeting*] at [*Time of meeting*] will be 100 percent effective. I have structured the agenda to provide optimum efficiency by presenting as much information about [*Topic of meeting*] as possible in the time allotted. This is one meeting you should not miss. I look forward to showing you my formula for success.

Sincerely yours,

[YOUR NAME]
[YOUR TITLE]

Confirmation of Order

[DATE]

[Mr./Mrs./Ms./Dr.] [CUSTOMER'S FULL NAME]
[CUSTOMER'S TITLE]
[COMPANY]
[ADDRESS]
[CITY], [STATE] [ZIP CODE]

Dear [Mr./Mrs./Ms./Dr.] [CUSTOMER'S LAST NAME]:

There is absolutely no reason to leave anything to chance. A little extra effort now decreases the chance that an error will occur later. My unwillingness to take unnecessary chances means that I must take direct responsibility for all my customer orders.

Therefore, I am confirming your order for [*Describe the order*] placed on [*Date order was placed*]. [YOUR COMPANY NAME] expects this order to be received by [COMPANY] no later than [*Number of days from the date the letter is sent* COMPANY *will receive order*] from today's date.

After double-checking with our department managers, I do not anticipate any changes that would delay the shipment. It has been a pleasure serving you. I look forward to working with [COMPANY] again to meet your [*General noun referring to (Describe the order), i.e., "advertising," "equipment," or "supplies"*] needs.

Sincerely yours,

[YOUR NAME]
[YOUR TITLE]

Confirmation of Speaker

[DATE]

[Mr./Mrs./Ms./Dr.] [FIRST AND LAST NAME]
[TITLE]
[COMPANY]
[ADDRESS]
[CITY], [STATE] [ZIP CODE]

Dear [Mr./Mrs./Ms./Dr.] [LAST NAME]:

Based on the tremendous response, our audience knows your reputation for engaging and entertaining, knowledge-filled presentations, so we look forward to filling the room with your voice and people eager to learn about [*Topic of speech*].

As a confirmation, [YOUR COMPANY NAME]'s conference is on [*Date of conference*] at [*Location of conference*] beginning at [*Time conference starts*]. Your speech is scheduled from [*Time person receiving letter starts speech*] to [*Time person receiving letter ends speech*]. Let me know if you need any special equipment such as a projector or VCR. I am confident that your involvement will help make this our most successful and enlightening event yet.

Sincerely yours,

[YOUR NAME]
[YOUR TITLE]

Conflict of Interest

TO: [*First and last name of person receiving memo*]

FROM: [YOUR NAME]
[YOUR TITLE]

DATE: [DATE]

SUBJECT: Conflict of Interest

Ethical standards are a key component of professionalism. Frequently, we must ask ourselves whether our actions will be beneficial to the entire company. [YOUR COMPANY NAME]'s employees have an obligation to practice business ethically, honestly, and unselfishly.

I recently learned that your affiliation with [*Name of company with which he/she has an affiliation*] could pose a potential conflict of interest in relation to your employment with [YOUR COMPANY NAME]. Conflict of interest covers many areas. In general, the term refers to situations in which an employee is in the position of disclosing information, influencing a decision, or partaking in a venture that results in personal gain.

Because you are innocent until proven guilty, I would like to hear your side of the story. Your relationship with [*Name of company with which he/she has an affiliation*] alone is not enough to create a conflict of interest. The rumors are circulating, and I want to stop them for the benefit of all concerned—you, me, [YOUR COMPANY NAME], and [*Name of company with which he/she has an affiliation*].

Whether or not you care to discuss the matter at length, I expect a response by [*Date by which you want person receiving memo to respond*]. Conflict of interest is a very sensitive matter that demands immediate attention.

cc: [COPIES TO]

Consulting Service Inquiry

[DATE]

[Mr./Mrs./Ms./Dr.] [FIRST AND LAST NAME]
[TITLE]
[COMPANY]
[ADDRESS]
[CITY], [STATE] [ZIP CODE]

Dear [Mr./Mrs./Ms./Dr.] [LAST NAME]:

To say we are better than other people is limiting. We all have talents in diverse areas. The key to success is recognizing the areas in which we lack talent and finding it elsewhere.

A metamorphosis that will require additional resources is underway at [YOUR COMPANY NAME]. Our management believes that [COMPANY] may be the vehicle taking us from where we are to where we plan to be. Please forward the following materials pertaining to your firm: company profile, client list, basic fee schedule, and professional references. This information can be sent to [YOUR COMPANY NAME *address*].

Give me a week or so to review the package before following up on our interest in [COMPANY]. Focusing on specialization has contributed greatly to our success. I look forward to learning if our professional goals and practices are complementary.

Sincerely yours,

[YOUR NAME]
[YOUR TITLE]

Continue Professional Education Request

TO: [*First and last name of person receiving memo*]

FROM: [YOUR NAME]
[YOUR TITLE]

DATE: [DATE]

SUBJECT: Continuing Professional Education Request Authorization

Knowledge and proficiency are key factors determining whether a challenge becomes an opportunity or a pitfall. Maximizing professional accomplishment through continuing education is easily neglected when business pressures climb. On the other hand, I have seen very real benefits result from classroom experiences.

I would like to pursue professional education that I think will further [YOUR COMPANY NAME]'s short- and long-range goals. I have spent time during the weekend and evening hours looking for reading material on [*Describe the type of professional education, i.e., "class," "conference," "seminar," etc's focus*]. While the bookstores and library offer a comprehensive selection, one cannot dispute the advantages of an instructor-directed curriculum.

I have found a [*Describe the type of professional education, i.e., "class," "conference," "seminar," etc*] that appears to be exactly what I need to increase my knowledge of [*Describe the type of professional education, i.e., "class," "conference," "seminar," etc's focus*]. After checking the work schedule, I have concluded that the class held [*Date(s) and time(s) classes will be held*] at [*Location of classes*] would be convenient for all concerned. The cost per student is fairly reasonable at $[*Dollar amount charged per student for the type of professional education, i.e., "class," "conference," "seminar," etc.*].

Upon receiving your positive reply, I will confirm my attendance and complete the required expense authorization forms. Thank you in advance for continuing to support my professional endeavors.

cc: [COPIES TO]

Contract Assignment

[DATE]

[Mr./Mrs./Ms./Dr.] [FIRST AND LAST NAME]
[TITLE]
[COMPANY]
[ADDRESS]
[CITY], [STATE] [ZIP CODE]

Dear [Mr./Mrs./Ms./Dr.] [LAST NAME]:

This letter serves as official notice that we have assigned all duties, obligations, performance requirements, and rights of our [*Name of the agreement*] Agreement, dated and executed on [*Date* YOUR COMPANY NAME *and* COMPANY *signed the agreement]*, to [*Name of company to which* YOUR COMPANY NAME *is assigning the agreement*] as of [*Date the contract is assigned*]. Therefore, [*Name of company to which* YOUR COMPANY NAME *is assigning the agreement*] has assumed fully our position in the agreement here and as above described.

I have enclosed a duplicate copy of this Contract Assignment notice for your signature to acknowledge receipt of this letter. Please return one signed original to my attention. If there are any questions, please do not hesitate to contact me. Thank you in advance for your prompt attention.

Sincerely yours,

[YOUR NAME]
[YOUR TITLE]

Agreed and Consented by:
[COMPANY]

Signature

____
Printed Name and Title

____
Date

Corporate Communications

TO: [*First and last name of person receiving memo*]

FROM: [YOUR NAME]
[YOUR TITLE]

DATE: [DATE]

SUBJECT: Organizational Hierarchy Facilitates Communication

Organizations build upon the literal definition of the word: a unit composed of many elements having specific functions that contribute collectively to the whole. There is no doubt that our individual efforts benefit all at [YOUR COMPANY NAME].

In an organization, various specialties create levels of authority and focus. One department understands its charter much better than another does, and vice versa. Therefore, corporate communications must work within established guidelines of authority.

All concerns, comments, and questions should be first directed to your immediate manager or supervisor. It is his or her responsibility to resolve the issue or seek additional support within the corporation at higher levels.

Should you believe your manager or supervisor is not taking every action to address your concern within a reasonable amount of time, you may contact [*Person responsible for handling policy enforcement*] for assistance. There are absolutely no exceptions to this policy.

Please direct any comments or questions regarding this policy to your immediate manager or supervisor. Thank you in advance for your respect of [YOUR COMPANY NAME]'s hierarchy and communication channels.

cc: [COPIES TO]

Court Action Potential

[DATE]

[Mr./Mrs./Ms./Dr.] [CUSTOMER'S FULL NAME]
[CUSTOMER'S TITLE]
[COMPANY]
[ADDRESS]
[CITY], [STATE] [ZIP CODE]

Dear [Mr./Mrs./Ms./Dr.] [CUSTOMER'S LAST NAME]:

Demand is hereby made upon [COMPANY] for the total amount of $[*Dollar amount of payment needed from* COMPANY] to satisfy all debts incurred for purchases made from our company. It is expected that [COMPANY] will remit full payment of $[*Dollar amount of payment needed from* COMPANY] on, or before, [*Date* COMPANY *must pay dollar amount of payment needed from* COMPANY *by*]. In accordance with the law, [YOUR COMPANY NAME] has notified the proper entities of [COMPANY]'s overdue debt, and we are prepared to take immediate action.

Although [YOUR COMPANY NAME] is reluctant to pursue such measures, we will have no choice if payment is not received before [*Date* COMPANY *must pay dollar amount of payment needed from* COMPANY *by*]. We hope for an immediate reconciliation in receiving what is rightfully ours before being forced to seek a harsher remedy.

Sincerely yours,

[YOUR NAME]
[YOUR TITLE]

Cover Letter for Bid

[DATE]

[Mr./Mrs./Ms./Dr.] [CUSTOMER'S FULL NAME]
[CUSTOMER'S TITLE]
[COMPANY]
[ADDRESS]
[CITY], [STATE] [ZIP CODE]

Dear [Mr./Mrs./Ms./Dr.] [CUSTOMER'S LAST NAME]:

It is a little known fact that for hundreds of years, the Chinese used gunpowder for fireworks. Wars were frequent, but the Chinese soldiers had no idea of the incredible power within their reach. Although they were familiar with gunpowder, they did not envision using that funny gray dust as a strategic weapon until China lay in ruins.

Business is a marketing war of bigger and better manufacturer claims. Vendor is pitted against vendor. While I am confident that there is no other choice in [COMPANY]'s bid request for [*Describe what the bid is for*], number [*Provide* COMPANY's *bid tracking number for what the bid is for*], than the enclosed, I admit to being biased by past success.

My professional experience advising clients just like [COMPANY] is marked by a long history of satisfied organizations. [YOUR COMPANY NAME] has the gunpowder; let's get together and use it as a strategic operational weapon. Joining forces with us is probably the best decision you can make for [COMPANY]'s future. We are the shortcut to prosperity and peace of mind.

Sincerely yours,

[YOUR NAME]
[YOUR TITLE]

Credit Bureau Report Request

[DATE]

[Mr./Mrs./Ms./Dr.] [FIRST AND LAST NAME]
[TITLE]
[COMPANY]
[ADDRESS]
[CITY], [STATE] [ZIP CODE]

Dear [Mr./Mrs./Ms./Dr.] [LAST NAME]:

Good habits are essential to personal and professional security. By controlling our lives, we actually become freer to enjoy additional experiences. The availability and extension of credit from one company to another is a perfect example.

[YOUR COMPANY NAME] does its homework and confirms that the people involved with us take their credit seriously. We need [COMPANY]'s help. We are requesting a complete credit profile and report on [*Customer* YOUR COMPANY NAME *needs the credit report on*], located at [*Address of Customer* YOUR COMPANY NAME *needs the credit report on]*, for the years [*Years* YOUR COMPANY NAME *wants information on*]. The release from [*Customer* YOUR COMPANY NAME *needs the credit report on*] authorizing and granting permission to [YOUR COMPANY NAME] to investigate their credit history is [*Most credit bureaus require authorization from the customer, i.e., "enclosed" or "granted on our credit application"*]. Please process payment for the credit report using [*Method* YOUR COMPANY NAME *is paying for report, i.e., "enclosed check" or "our credit bureau account"*].

Business cannot afford to extend credit frivolously or to those who have not developed good track records. Thank you for your help in picking the winners.

[YOUR TITLE]

Credit for Return

[DATE]

[Mr./Mrs./Ms./Dr.] [CUSTOMER'S FULL NAME]
[CUSTOMER'S TITLE]
[COMPANY]
[ADDRESS]
[CITY], [STATE] [ZIP CODE]

Dear [Mr./Mrs./Ms./Dr.] [CUSTOMER'S LAST NAME]:

Some people believe life would be easier if we all had the same likes and dislikes. Communication would be all but unnecessary, and marketing a snap. But we are all different. Communication sometimes breaks down, mass marketing sometimes fails to do its job, and merchandise is occasionally returned.

We recently received [*Name of product returned*], which apparently did not meet [COMPANY]'s requirements. Therefore, we are posting to your account a credit for $[*Amount* COMPANY *paid for name of product returned*], the amount paid.

Please accept our apologies for your apparent lack of satisfaction with this one product. Although we try to give our customers the best of all worlds, uniqueness challenges these efforts. [YOUR COMPANY NAME] looks forward to having the opportunity to fulfill other [COMPANY] needs.

Sincerely yours,

[YOUR NAME]
[YOUR TITLE]

Credit Inquiry

[DATE]

[Mr./Mrs./Ms./Dr.] [FIRST AND LAST NAME]
[TITLE]
[COMPANY]
[ADDRESS]
[CITY], [STATE] [ZIP CODE]

Dear [Mr./Mrs./Ms./Dr.] [LAST NAME]:

I always like to know where I stand. Having a complete understanding of where one is enables proactive decision making. Change for the sake of change is not as beneficial as change that is planned. In preparation for making financial moves promoting our imminent growth, [YOUR COMPANY NAME] needs your help.

We are requesting a complete report of our credit history with [COMPANY] over the past [*Period credit inquiry report should cover*], including the following: available line of credit; average, highest, and lowest balances; length of time the account has been active; number of times, if any, a late payment has been made; and outstanding amount due on the account. The above pertains to account number [YOUR COMPANY NAME's *credit account number assigned by* COMPANY].

As [YOUR COMPANY NAME] continues to take advantage of tremendous opportunities, your information facilitates business planning. My target date for receiving the report is [*Date the* COMPANY *should provide credit inquiry report*]. I realize that this may be short notice, and I want you to know that your assistance is appreciated. I look forward to [COMPANY]'s continued participation in our company's growth.

Sincerely yours,

[YOUR NAME]
[YOUR TITLE]

Credit Referral Request

[DATE]

[Mr./Mrs./Ms./Dr.] [FIRST AND LAST NAME]
[TITLE]
[COMPANY]
[ADDRESS]
[CITY], [STATE] [ZIP CODE]

Dear [Mr./Mrs./Ms./Dr.] [LAST NAME]:

Whether beginning a business or embarking on adulthood, minimizing risks increases the potential for achievement. The groundwork established pushes us to the next plateau. Suddenly, we realize that risk is necessary, and we must decide how much risk we are willing to take.

[YOUR COMPANY NAME] investigates the risk factor associated with every client who requests credit. The more information we can obtain about a client's past dealings, the better equipped we are to make decisions about his creditworthiness.

We were given [COMPANY]'s name as a reference by [*Customer* YOUR COMPANY NAME *wants information on*]. Your information is crucial to our decision. In accordance with applicable laws, the areas about which we seek information are as follows: available line of credit; average, highest, and lowest balances; length of time the account has been active; number of times, if any, a late payment has been made; and outstanding amount due on the account. The above pertains to account number [*Customer's account number with* COMPANY].

You can forward this information to [*First and last name of person at* YOUR COMPANY NAME *who should receive information, or if yourself, "me"*]. Thank you for your assistance. From one business veteran to another, I appreciate your professional courtesy and prompt reply. We both know risk minimization assists profit maximization.

Sincerely yours,

[YOUR NAME]
[YOUR TITLE]

Credit Referral Response

[DATE]

[Mr./Mrs./Ms./Dr.] [FIRST AND LAST NAME]
[TITLE]
[COMPANY]
[ADDRESS]
[CITY], [STATE] [ZIP CODE]

Dear [Mr./Mrs./Ms./Dr.] [LAST NAME]:

Success often begets success. In our years of business, [YOUR COMPANY NAME] has prospered by adhering to the Golden Rule. Every kind gesture is returned eventually; in other words, what goes around comes around.

The credit reference for [*Customer* COMPANY *needs the credit information on*] submitted by your company is my responsibility. As a professional, clearly you realize that the Consumer Protection Act and other statutes legally limit the information about a business or individual's credit and payment history that can be disclosed.

Therefore, in accordance with the law, we provide the following credit facts for [CUSTOMER COMPANY *needs the credit information on*], located at [*Address of* CUSTOMER COMPANY], for the past [*Years* CUSTOMER COMPANY *information pertains to*]: [*Credit information for* CUSTOMER COMPANY *needs the credit information on*]. Having this knowledge about our experience with [CUSTOMER COMPANY *needs the credit information on*] should assist in [COMPANY]'s decision and success. If there are any questions, please do hesitate to contact me. It is my pleasure to help another company achieve its profit potential.

Sincerely yours,

[YOUR NAME]
[YOUR TITLE]

Customer Misunderstood Delivery Terms

[DATE]

[Mr./Mrs./Ms./Dr.] [CUSTOMER'S FULL NAME]
[CUSTOMER'S TITLE]
[COMPANY]
[ADDRESS]
[CITY], [STATE] [ZIP CODE]

Dear [Mr./Mrs./Ms./Dr.] [CUSTOMER'S LAST NAME]:

No matter what, where, or how we buy, it takes time and energy. Business is pressure-filled enough without vendors adding to the stress. [YOUR COMPANY NAME] is committed to making buying from us effortless not just the first time, but every time.

Our total quality assurance program safeguards all customer commitments. From initial sale to final delivery, rules are in place and printed on the literature all customers receive. Your recent letter expressed disappointment regarding the delivery of our products.

I understand your position. However, our [YOUR COMPANY NAME *literature enclosed with letter, i.e., "brochure," "catalog," etc. that specifies delivery terms*] clearly states that goods are delivered by [*Describe means and method by which orders are delivered*] within [*Length of time* YOUR COMPANY NAME *guarantees delivery by*]. [COMPANY]'s transaction meets these criteria. Enclosed is a copy of [*Name of* YOUR COMPANY NAME *literature enclosed with letter, i.e., "brochure," "catalog," etc. that specifies delivery terms*] for your review and to eliminate any future misunderstanding. If you still question whether the policy was followed, do not hesitate to call. You can depend on me to put your best interest ahead of mine.

Sincerely yours,

[YOUR NAME]
[YOUR TITLE]

Customer Misunderstood Sale Terms

[DATE]

[Mr./Mrs./Ms./Dr.] [CUSTOMER'S FULL NAME]
[CUSTOMER'S TITLE]
[COMPANY]
[ADDRESS]
[CITY], [STATE] [ZIP CODE]

Dear [Mr./Mrs./Ms./Dr.] [CUSTOMER'S LAST NAME]:

Tell a child a secret, and watch his or her eyes light up with joy. In business though, secrecy can severely damage customer relationships. For as long as [YOUR COMPANY NAME] has been in business, ethical practices have guided our dealings with both customers and employees.

Sometimes in our buying enthusiasm and desire to act quickly, we overlook details. [YOUR COMPANY NAME] takes extra time to describe company policies that relate to purchases. Our [*Name of* YOUR COMPANY NAME *literature enclosed with letter, i.e., "brochure," "catalog," etc. that specifies sale terms*] exemplifies our commitment to ethical business practices. Included in it are the following statements: [*Describe buying terms as related to* COMPANY's *complaint*].

I have enclosed a copy of [*Name of* YOUR COMPANY NAME *literature enclosed with letter, i.e., "brochure," "catalog," etc. that specifies sale terms*] for your review. [YOUR COMPANY NAME] is a trustworthy company in a sometimes untrustworthy world. If any doubts remain, please do not hesitate one moment in contacting me. [YOUR COMPANY NAME] is proud of the honorable reputation that keeps customers coming back.

Sincerely yours,

[YOUR NAME]
[YOUR TITLE]

Dealing With Reporters

TO: [*First and last name of person receiving memo*]

FROM: [YOUR NAME]
[YOUR TITLE]

DATE: [DATE]

SUBJECT: Dealing with Broadcast and Print Reporters

Literally thousands of men and women in our country are charged with the task of keeping the public up to date on happenings in the world. Because of their efforts, we can pick up a newspaper or watch television and become more aware of life as it is today and will be tomorrow. Reporters have a difficult job getting accurate information and then condensing their research to fit in the time or space allotted.

Frequently, media people, whose titles include reporter, editor, researcher, reviewer, and publisher, call upon people like us for information or interviews. We may have specialized knowledge that will help them improve their stories.

To ensure accuracy of information and for the protection of our employees, [YOUR COMPANY NAME] has established one point of contact for media-related people. All inquiries by media personnel, whether written or oral, should be directed immediately to [*First and last name of person responsible for media-related communications*] at [*Telephone number for the person responsible for media-related communications*].

There are absolutely no exceptions to this procedure. Thank you for recognizing the importance of this matter. Your compliance is a personal and professional obligation to maintain the highest integrity of our employees and company.

cc: [COPIES TO]

Decline PR Interview

[DATE]

[Mr./Mrs./Ms./Dr.] [FIRST AND LAST NAME]
[TITLE]
[COMPANY]
[ADDRESS]
[CITY], [STATE] [ZIP CODE]

Dear [Mr./Mrs./Ms./Dr.] [LAST NAME]:

The timing of events is very important in life. We seem either to need more time or to lose patience waiting for the "right" time. I realize that your deadline for the story on [YOUR COMPANY NAME] is approaching, and I appreciate the confidence and interest in our company that your request for an interview demonstrates.

Our company takes pleasure in assisting others in their professional quests. However, the timing is very inappropriate and forces me to decline your request.

I do not wish to dampen your enthusiasm, so keep [YOUR COMPANY NAME] in mind for a future story. Best wishes for success in your endeavor. I hope to hear from you in the future when the timing may be better.

Sincerely yours,

[YOUR NAME]
[YOUR TITLE]

Declining to Respond

[DATE]

[Mr./Mrs./Ms./Dr.] [CUSTOMER'S FULL NAME]
[CUSTOMER'S TITLE]
[COMPANY]
[ADDRESS]
[CITY], [STATE] [ZIP CODE]

Dear [Mr./Mrs./Ms./Dr.] [CUSTOMER'S LAST NAME]:

Preserving a reputation for excellence is demanding. After reviewing [COMPANY]'s bid for [*Describe what the bid was for*], number [*Provide* COMPANY'S *bid tracking number for and describe what the bid was for*], we were faced with a difficult decision. Of course, we want the opportunity, but we are not sure that we can adhere to our usual high quality standards.

It is a painstaking process to turn down potential business. Unfortunately, this letter is formal notification that [YOUR COMPANY NAME] is not responding to the aforementioned bid. Please do not interpret this as a lack of desire to establish a long-term relationship with [COMPANY].

[YOUR COMPANY NAME] hopes that other opportunities more in line with our areas of expertise and specialization will materialize. Then, we have the chance to demonstrate our unparalleled dedication and professionalism. I look forward to those opportunities and extend our entire company's thanks for keeping us in your future. [YOUR COMPANY NAME] is the most trusted name in the [*Describe* YOUR COMPANY NAME's *main business emphasis*] business. We are committed to staying that way, even if it means forsaking an opportunity.

Sincerely yours,

[YOUR NAME]
[YOUR TITLE]

Decreased Earnings

TO: [*First and last name of person receiving memo*]

FROM: [YOUR NAME]
[YOUR TITLE]

DATE: [DATE]

SUBJECT: Reduction in Corporate Earnings

Business enterprise is a work-in-process created by the hands of economic and market conditions. As the form takes shape, differing opinions on the right or wrong placement of angles and shading are inevitable. It takes vision to see the big picture.

Likewise, [YOUR COMPANY NAME] is in a development stage that requires a shift of resources. Our assets are many, yet new and exciting projects require funding. These are adding value to our future while reducing corporate earnings.

It is not uncommon for earnings to decrease as a business assumes the form needed for a prosperous future. We have all the human resources and technological tools needed to be a master in our industry. More time is the only thing required to finish this work of art.

cc: [COPIES TO]

Delayed Shipment of Product

TO: [*First and last name of person receiving memo*]

FROM: [YOUR NAME]
[YOUR TITLE]

DATE: [DATE]

SUBJECT: Delayed Shipments of [*Name of product delayed*]

Salespeople speak of good times when product demand exceeds supply. Economists worry about unbalanced scales. Manufacturing goes into overdrive, and we must be prepared for the delay.

The volume of customer orders for [*Name of product delayed*] has both positive and negative effects. Communication is the key to handling all aspects of this delay. I would like each of you to take a personal interest in maintaining our corporate customer satisfaction standards.

Check your files and advise those customers with pending orders that we are taking all steps necessary to complete these as quickly as possible. Although it is not feasible to provide a firm date, we anticipate being able to fulfill requests for [*Name of product delayed*] by [*Date the product orders can be filled*]. Please let me know of any disgruntled customer responses to the news, and thanks for your assistance in the matter.

cc: [COPIES TO]

Delayed Shipment to Customer

[DATE]

[Mr./Mrs./Ms./Dr.] [CUSTOMER'S FULL NAME]
[CUSTOMER'S TITLE]
[COMPANY]
[ADDRESS]
[CITY], [STATE] [ZIP CODE]

Dear [Mr./Mrs./Ms./Dr.] [CUSTOMER'S LAST NAME]:

It's easy to say, "plan for the future or be doomed to live in the past." Forecasting customer needs in today's dynamic marketplace is a complex science. While we know that [*Name of product ordered*]'s quality and price are superior, the volume of customer orders surprised us and exceeded our in-stock supply.

Moving quickly, we have taken every action possible to limit any inconvenience to our customers. It is our intention to complete your order for [*Name of product ordered*] by [*Date* YOUR COMPANY NAME *plans to ship product ordered*].

[YOUR COMPANY NAME] is confident that our future forecasts, now based on past success, will be more accurate. Thank you for your understanding and making our success possible with your ongoing support. We plan to continue being the undisputed leader in [*Describe* YOUR COMPANY NAME's *main business emphasis*], but now we are smarter and better than ever before.

Sincerely yours,

[YOUR NAME]
[YOUR TITLE]

Demand for Retraction

[DATE]

[Mr./Mrs./Ms./Dr.] [FIRST AND LAST NAME]
[TITLE]
[COMPANY]
[ADDRESS]
[CITY], [STATE] [ZIP CODE]

Dear [Mr./Mrs./Ms./Dr.] [LAST NAME]:

Censorship was predictable in the old Soviet Union when the government controlled the official newspaper, Pravda. Rarely were both sides of a story revealed. Since 1776 when our great nation was founded, however, Americans have not tolerated censorship.

I must tell you that while reading the article about our company, [YOUR COMPANY NAME], printed in the [*Date of publication*] issue of [COMPANY], I expected soldiers to come stomping through the door at any moment. The article written by [*First and last name of author*] is clearly an example of regulated editing and/or writing. Half-a-truth is half-a-lie.

Specifically, "[*Select what you consider the worst sentence(s) from article*]," is sensationalist journalism. The coverage could have been made accurate by including [*Describe and list by number things that should have been included in article*].

In the interest of fairness, [YOUR COMPANY NAME] demands that [COMPANY] print an immediate retraction or clarification of the aforementioned article. On behalf of [YOUR COMPANY NAME], I will be looking for justice and hoping that future dealings with [COMPANY] do not give me the Siberian chills.

Sincerely yours,

[YOUR NAME]
[YOUR TITLE]

Deny a Rumor

[DATE]

[Mr./Mrs./Ms./Dr.] [FIRST AND LAST NAME]
[TITLE]
[COMPANY]
[ADDRESS]
[CITY], [STATE] [ZIP CODE]

Dear [Mr./Mrs./Ms./Dr.] [LAST NAME]:

The children's game of telephone is designed to demonstrate how rumors get started. In the game, a story is told to the first person, who tells it to the second, and so on, until the last person in line is asked to announce what he or she heard. The last person's version of the original story invariably causes laughter among the game's participants.

When paraphrased, any piece of information tends to lose accuracy. The story changes or is embellished; facts are left out as it moves from person to person. Having recently become aware of a rumor about [YOUR COMPANY NAME], I wish to stop it before the damage is too great to be repaired. There is absolutely no truth to the rumor that [*Describe the obvious lie in the rumor*]. As we both know, words carry many meanings, and rumors are often spread for selfish purposes. I hope that this letter makes it clear that the hearsay is not our say.

Sincerely yours,

[YOUR NAME]
[YOUR TITLE]

Discount Request

[DATE]

[Mr./Mrs./Ms./Dr.] [FIRST AND LAST NAME]
[TITLE]
[COMPANY]
[ADDRESS]
[CITY], [STATE] [ZIP CODE]

Dear [Mr./Mrs./Ms./Dr.] [LAST NAME]:

The airline industry has benefited tremendously from a reward system for frequent flyers. "Travel with us now and you get free flights later," the advertisements proclaim. [YOUR COMPANY NAME]'s account with [COMPANY] clearly exhibits many long trips at first class fares.

As a dedicated customer, we have a special request of [COMPANY]. The current economy forces us to become lean and mean in our competitive stance. In cutting corners, we must limit expenditures that probably include future [COMPANY] purchases.

Based on our relationship, it is my hope that [COMPANY] will help us with our cost-saving measures. [YOUR COMPANY NAME] requests that future purchases be discounted by industry standards. Thank you for your consideration and reply. Think of it as a frequent flyer program rewarding us for the thousands of miles we have flown exclusively with [COMPANY].

Sincerely yours,

[YOUR NAME]
[YOUR TITLE]

Discussion Appeal

[DATE]

[Mr./Mrs./Ms./Dr.] [CUSTOMER'S FULL NAME]
[CUSTOMER'S TITLE]
[COMPANY]
[ADDRESS]
[CITY], [STATE] [ZIP CODE]

Dear [Mr./Mrs./Ms./Dr.] [CUSTOMER'S LAST NAME]:

When things are going badly, we tend to turn our backs on the world and refuse to deal with the issues that haunt us. [COMPANY] has always been a valued [YOUR COMPANY NAME] customer, and we are confused by the change in your payment history. I have checked the files for any circumstances that might explain such unprofessionalism.

There are none. The file is, however, full of our requests for an explanation or partial payment. I also see a fair number of unfulfilled [COMPANY] promises. The account is $[*Dollar amount of payment needed from* COMPANY] overdue, which means that it will soon be turned over to a collection agency.

To date, I have personally gone out of my way to see that such action is not taken with [COMPANY]. Why? Because a careful review of your payment history suggests that this is not your normal business practice.

I must know what is going on and what type of payment, if any, [COMPANY] will remit on the account immediately. Why can't we discuss this issue before I am forced to turn the account over for collection? One action taken by [COMPANY] could prevent [YOUR COMPANY NAME] from taking any. I am not your enemy; I hope to hear from you soon.

Sincerely yours,

[YOUR NAME]
[YOUR TITLE]

Drug Test Program

TO: All Staff

FROM: [YOUR NAME]
[YOUR TITLE]

DATE: [DATE]

SUBJECT: Drug Testing Program

A good work environment clearly includes much more than the right supplies or the latest and greatest equipment. While these are vital, outfitting the office and having good people are not mutually exclusive goals. One clearly depends on the other for an efficient, productive, and safe environment.

[YOUR COMPANY NAME] is committed to providing a healthy atmosphere for all employees. We never stop searching for ways to better ourselves, whether through additional resources or continuing education programs. In keeping with this philosophy, we want all team members to be aware that they, too, affect the work environment personally and professionally. Therefore, any employee or job applicant may be requested to provide body substance samples (e.g., blood, urine) to be tested for the presence of alcohol, amphetamines, cocaine, marijuana, opiates, and phencyclidine (PCP). Positive test results will lead to employment reassessment and/or rehabilitation. Any questions about [YOUR COMPANY NAME]'s drug testing policy and program should be directed to [*Name of person responsible for drug testing program*].

Illegal drug use has no place in any part of our lives. Drugs have proved repeatedly to be a destructive force in the user's personal and professional relationships. [YOUR COMPANY NAME] is a strong enforcer and proponent of a drug-free environment.

cc: [COPIES TO]

Due Date Extension Request

[DATE]

[Mr./Mrs./Ms./Dr.] [CUSTOMER'S FULL NAME]
[CUSTOMER'S TITLE]
[COMPANY]
[ADDRESS]
[CITY], [STATE] [ZIP CODE]

Dear [Mr./Mrs./Ms./Dr.] [CUSTOMER'S LAST NAME]:

[COMPANY] has presented us with a unique challenge. I have spent much time formulating a time-based action plan to be used in completing the bid for [*Describe what the bid is for*], number [*Provide* COMPANY's *bid tracking number for what the bid is for*]. Resources have been distributed with the obvious goal of winning your business.

[YOUR COMPANY NAME] has a reputation for delivering superb bid responses to its customers. I fear that submitting anything less may jeopardize my, and the company's, professional standing. In order for us to uphold this standard, [YOUR COMPANY NAME] requests an extension of the due date from [*Date* COMPANY's *bid is due*] to [*Date* YOUR COMPANY NAME *wants to submit the bid response].*

The extra time will permit us to deliver a document worthy of your business and praise. If possible, please confirm this extension in writing at your earliest convenience. Thank you for your professional courtesy in this matter. I consider a bid response more than a document; it is a direct reflection of [YOUR COMPANY NAME]'s customer commitment.

Sincerely yours,

[YOUR NAME]
[YOUR TITLE]

Early Termination of Lease

[DATE]

[Mr./Mrs./Ms./Dr.] [FIRST AND LAST NAME]
[TITLE]
[COMPANY]
[ADDRESS]
[CITY], [STATE] [ZIP CODE]

Dear [Mr./Mrs./Ms./Dr.] [LAST NAME]:

Fundamentally, business is a dynamic entity whose plans made in good faith are subject to laws of economic warfare. [YOUR COMPANY NAME]'s battlefield position and other extenuating circumstances require an immediate change in plans. Much to my regret, I am forced to realign the troops in a considerably smaller location.

After extensive review, we have no alternative but to relocate effective [*Number of days* YOUR COMPANY NAME *is moving from date letter sent*] days from today's date. The entire [COMPANY] has been so professional in the past that I wanted to tell you just as soon as this unfortunate decision was made. In addition, we understand that our move affects the building's management. Please know our office is open to prospective tenants during normal business hours.

If you need to conduct tours over weekends, we will be happy to accommodate you; it is the least we can do in return for your professional consideration in this matter. [*First name of person receiving letter*], thank you for all you have done for [YOUR COMPANY NAME].

Sincerely yours,

[YOUR NAME]
[YOUR TITLE]

Elected Official Assistance Request

[DATE]

The Honorable [FIRST and LAST NAME]
[TITLE]
[COMPANY]
[ADDRESS]
[CITY], [STATE] [ZIP CODE]

Dear [Mr./Mrs./Ms./Dr.] [LAST NAME]:

The truth is, the word "government" brings to mind scenes of officials caught too deep in bureaucracy's maze to accomplish much of anything. Paperwork and more paperwork leaves businesses like [YOUR COMPANY NAME] speechless except for the voices elected to represent us. Caught in government's quagmire, I seek your personal and professional involvement in resolving a specific problem.

So far, efforts to [*Describe the problem*] have resulted in nothing but frustration and obstruction. Moving from one department to another, [YOUR COMPANY NAME] has been repeatedly told, "I don't handle that. You need to talk to so-and-so."There appears to be nothing left to do but take both of our valuable time through this letter.

The bottom line is that I need your help to [*Describe the problem's resolution*]. From what I understand, the following actions must be taken: [*Describe and list by number steps needed for the problem's resolution to occur*]. Clearly, this problem is not insurmountable if we keep the channels of communication open.

[*First name of person receiving letter*], I am confident that our request is quite reasonable when both sides of the story are fully understood. On behalf of [YOUR COMPANY NAME], I appreciate your assistance in settling the matter quickly. It is my hope that either you or a staff member can cut through the bureaucracy and speak loudly on our behalf.

Sincerely yours,

[YOUR NAME]
[YOUR TITLE]

Employee Anniversary

TO: [*First and last name of person receiving memo*]

FROM: [YOUR NAME]
[YOUR TITLE]

DATE: [DATE]

SUBJECT: Your Employment Anniversary

Jukeboxes and the twist faded into obscurity, and poodle skirts lost their glamour. In the following decades, the nation saw everything from peace movements to combat as we moved from the atomic age into the information age. Change is inherent in life's progression.

Helping [YOUR COMPANY NAME] maneuver through past and present trends, you have been a reassuring guiding force over the past [*Number of years of first and last name of person receiving memo has been employed*] years of your employment. Don't think for a moment that we could have become what we are today without your skills and talents. From those very first days, you have been a major contributor to [YOUR COMPANY NAME]'s prosperity.

Then, as now, your ideas and steadfast devotion to excellence pervade our entire organization. Please accept as a small token of our appreciation, recognizing your [*Number of years of first and last name of person receiving memo has been employed*] years of service, our gift of [*Details of the anniversary gift*]. This is truly a celebration, and we look forward to many more in the future. Thank you for being a reliable team member who possesses talents that will never go out of style.

cc: [COPIES TO]

Employee Conduct

TO: [*First and last name of person receiving memo*]

FROM: [YOUR NAME]
[YOUR TITLE]

DATE: [DATE]

SUBJECT: Employee Conduct Reminder

Regulations are an important part of our lives. Everywhere we turn, a custom or a guideline dictates acceptable behavior. Whether we personally believe in the soundness of this or that rule, we must believe that most rules were created with the best interests of the majority in mind.

[YOUR COMPANY NAME] has rules that govern every employee's conduct. These rules were made to benefit every member of our team, but it seems that some team members may have forgotten the importance of playing by the rules. Therefore, I highlight the areas where memory loss seems greatest.

[YOUR COMPANY NAME] employee conduct rules include but are not limited to the following: [*Describe rules needing reinforcement*]. A complete list with explanations is available from [*First and last name of person having the rule list*].

There are absolutely no exceptions to our rules, and failure to comply may result in disciplinary action. If you see team rules being broken, notify [*First and last name of person responsible for enforcing the rules*] at [*Telephone number for person responsible for enforcing the rules*]. Such reports are held in strict confidence, so you need not fear reprisal. The confidentiality rule, like the others, is for everyone's benefit. Thank you for reminding yourself and co-workers of [YOUR COMPANY NAME]'s rules of conduct.

cc: [COPIES TO]

Employee Death

TO: [*First and last name of person receiving memo*]

FROM: [YOUR NAME]
[YOUR TITLE]

DATE: [DATE]

SUBJECT: The Death of [*First and last name of person who died*]

When the ties of friendship and camaraderie are abruptly severed, faith and strength lighten the load of our pain. Grief can be the greatest of teachers, allowing us to have more compassion for our fellow man. Death rekindles in us the very essence and importance of life sometimes left behind in our youth.

We were lucky to have had [*First and last name of person who died*] touch us and be part of our lives. [*Pronoun referring to deceased person's gender, i.e., "his" or "her,"*] laughter and smile remain now as we bow our heads in sorrow. [*First name of person who died*] will remain with us for many years to come in our thoughts and words. If you would like to send your condolences to [*First name of person who died*]'s family, let me know.

I am sure the family would appreciate knowing how much we miss their loved one. And take a moment today to reflect on what is important in your life. To say we were wronged by so-and-so or this person has more than I do is trivial in loss's pain. While we cannot quickly overcome the grief we feel, perhaps we can learn to cherish our life a little more every day.

cc: [COPIES TO]

Employee Family Death

TO: [*First and last name of person receiving memo*]

FROM: [YOUR NAME]
[YOUR TITLE]

DATE: [DATE]

SUBJECT: Our Deepest Sympathies

As night's darkness is followed by dawn, sorrow is followed by comfort. Please know that your [YOUR COMPANY NAME] family extends its deepest, most heartfelt sympathies on the death of your beloved [*Relationship of person who died, i.e., "brother," "child," "father," "mother," "sister," etc.*].

There is not one among us who has not suffered the trauma of a death sometime in our lives. Most have found comfort in paying the ultimate homage to a person who was dear to them. This is to take the characteristics we cherished the most in the departed loved one and pass them on for the benefit of others. If there is anything we can do to lessen your pain, remember we are here to help.

cc: [COPIES TO]

Employee of the Month Announcement

TO: [*First and last name of person receiving memo*]

FROM: [YOUR NAME]
[YOUR TITLE]

DATE: [DATE]

SUBJECT: We're Looking for the Employee of the Month

"Passing the buck" was first described by Mark Twain in 1872. During early American card games, a piece of buckskin was passed from player to player indicating the one who was next in line to deal. The phrase referred only to a shift in duty with no hidden meaning.

Today, passing the buck has a negative connotation that is incompatible with [YOUR COMPANY NAME]'s team spirit. We want our players to help one another strive to meet individual and department goals. Whether through a seemingly small or easily recognizable effort, a day does not go by without someone in our company going the extra mile for everyone's benefit.

We thank those special employees for their inspiring actions every month through our Employee of the Month Award. These people don't believe in passing the buck and regularly perform beyond all expectations in their job descriptions. Their careers encompass more than the duties outlined on a piece of paper.

Soon, you will be receiving a nomination form that will help us select the recipient of [YOUR COMPANY NAME]'s Employee of the Month Award. Winners are given [*List what award recipient receives*]. Think about how you could win and put those thoughts into action not just today but every day. Passing the buck is best left in card games and out of our professional careers.

cc: [COPIES TO]

Employee of the Month Recipient

TO: [*First and last name of person receiving memo*]

FROM: [YOUR NAME]
[YOUR TITLE]

DATE: [DATE]

SUBJECT: [*First and last name of award recipient*] Receives Employee of the Month Award

Being average is no longer good enough in this competitive world. Information flows and market conditions change faster than ever before.

To continue meeting [YOUR COMPANY NAME] goals, we are taking a proactive position. Promoting above average performance continues monthly in the recognition of special team members with our Employee of the Month Award. It gives me great pleasure to welcome [*First and last name of award recipient*] into our [YOUR COMPANY NAME] achiever's Hall of Fame for the month of [*Month awarded*].

Time after time, [*Pronoun referring to recipient's gender, i.e., "he" or "she," "his" or "her"*] has taken the initiative in promoting the highest standards of team activities. A listing of every contribution [*First and last name of award recipient*] has made to our company would take many pages. The nominations drew particular attention to [*Pronoun referring to recipient's gender, i.e., "he" or "she," "his" or "her"*] efforts in [*Describe the reason award recipient won award*].

Join me today in personally congratulating [*First and last name of award recipient*] for a winning performance. Mediocrity certainly has no place in [*Pronoun referring to recipient's gender, i.e., "he" or "she," "his" or "her"*] vocabulary.

cc: [COPIES TO]

Employee Rude Apology

[DATE]

[Mr./Mrs./Ms./Dr.] [CUSTOMER'S FULL NAME]
[CUSTOMER'S TITLE]
[COMPANY]
[ADDRESS]
[CITY], [STATE] [ZIP CODE]

Dear [Mr./Mrs./Ms./Dr.] [CUSTOMER'S LAST NAME]:

There is absolutely no excuse for rudeness in the home or workplace. A little kindness goes a long way. We at [YOUR COMPANY NAME] pride ourselves on the good customer relations that allow companies like [COMPANY] to turn to us with confidence.

To say that I am disturbed about the incident regarding [*Describe what* COMPANY *was doing when incident happened*] is an understatement. The situation was examined thoroughly, and the strictest reprimands enforced. [*First name of person receiving letter*], I ask you to remember that the actions of one person do not reflect the attitude of our entire company. Thank you for your tolerance in the matter. Hopefully, we can move forward and put the past far behind us.

Sincerely yours,

[YOUR NAME]
[YOUR TITLE]

Employment Offer

[DATE]

[Mr./Mrs./Ms./Dr.] [FIRST AND LAST NAME]
[ADDRESS]
[CITY], [STATE] [ZIP CODE]

Dear [Mr./Mrs./Ms./Dr.] [LAST NAME]:

Ability alone does not lead to achievement. Enthusiasm, knowledge, perseverance, and unity promote success. Because you possess these characteristics, [YOUR COMPANY NAME] is pleased to extend an offer to join our talented staff as a [*Title of position offered to person receiving letter*] beginning on [*Start date of employment*].

In this position, you will be responsible for [*Describe and list by number responsibilities of and title of position offered to person receiving letter*]. Clearly, this is an incredible opportunity to utilize and develop your professional skills. The compensation of $[*Dollar amount paid*] per [*Length of time, i.e., "hour," "month," "week," or "year"*] is quite competitive in today's market.

In addition, you will be eligible for bonuses and salary increases. [YOUR COMPANY NAME] rewards individual and team achievement based on the results of performance appraisals conducted every [*Interval at which performance appraisals are conducted*]. I look forward to your acceptance of this offer and to welcoming you into [YOUR COMPANY NAME]'s team of professionals.

Sincerely yours,

[YOUR NAME]
[YOUR TITLE]

Enclosed Contract

[DATE]

[Mr./Mrs./Ms./Dr.] [CUSTOMER'S FULL NAME]
[CUSTOMER'S TITLE]
[COMPANY]
[ADDRESS]
[CITY], [STATE] [ZIP CODE]

Dear [Mr./Mrs./Ms./Dr.] [CUSTOMER'S LAST NAME]:

Good companies welcome the opportunity to put their commitments in writing. Agreements protect the interests of both parties. Thank you for your help in preparing the contract for [*Describe what the contract is for*] being executed between [COMPANY] and [YOUR COMPANY NAME]. I know it took a lot of time and patience.

Although the enclosed documents are direct results of our previous discussions, please review them thoroughly. I have verified that the contract contains your primary concerns of [*Describe highlights of contract*]. Just sign on page [*Page number of contract COMPANY must sign*], and your long-awaited solution for [*Describe the contract's purpose*] is within reach.

On behalf of [YOUR COMPANY NAME], thank you again for your assistance in making our business relationship possible. I look forward to getting started on meeting [COMPANY]'s requirements.

Sincerely yours,

[YOUR NAME]
[YOUR TITLE]

Enjoyed Speech

[DATE]

[Mr./Mrs./Ms./Dr.] [CUSTOMER'S FULL NAME]
[CUSTOMER'S TITLE]
[COMPANY]
[ADDRESS]
[CITY], [STATE] [ZIP CODE]

Dear [Mr./Mrs./Ms./Dr.] [CUSTOMER'S LAST NAME]:

It takes ability, knowledge, and talent to express ideas in a way that is both informative and entertaining. I feel fortunate to have had the opportunity to hear your recent speech about [*Describe the subject of the speech*]. From the introduction to the closing remarks, the content was helpful and right on the money.

An audience's reaction is a speaker's best indicator of success. In addition to keeping our attention, your thoughts stimulated further thinking on the subject. You must find great satisfaction in being revered so highly.

Congratulations on your apparent success, and please let me know when and where you speak next. Other professionals in my contact circle would definitely enjoy your presentation as much as I did. I wish you continued success in all your endeavors!

Sincerely yours,

[YOUR NAME]
[YOUR TITLE]

Equal Employment Opportunity

TO: All Staff

FROM: [YOUR NAME]
[YOUR TITLE]

DATE: [DATE]

SUBJECT: Equal Employment Opportunity

In creating a bona fide democracy, our founding fathers established justice as one of the rights to which citizens of this country are entitled. Today, more than 200 years later, [YOUR COMPANY NAME] reaffirms its commitment to equality and fairness.

All advancement and employment decisions are based on ability, merit, and qualification. Employee relations are not influenced in any manner by an employee or applicant's age, color, disability, national origin, race, religion, or sex. Our affirmative action program further promotes equality throughout the organization.

Should you have any questions or concerns about [YOUR COMPANY NAME]'s commitment to equal employment opportunities, please bring them to the immediate attention of [*First and last name of person responsible in human resources or personnel*]. All reports are held in the strictest confidence. Thank you for your assistance in promoting fairness and equality throughout [YOUR COMPANY NAME].

cc: [COPIES TO]

Equipment Purchase Request

TO: [*First and last name of person receiving memo*]

FROM: [YOUR NAME]
[YOUR TITLE]

DATE: [DATE]

SUBJECT: Request Authorization to Purchase [*Describe equipment requested, i.e., "computer," "copier," "fax machine," "printer," etc*]

Attempting to do a job without the right equipment is frustrating at best. Patience wears thin as the deadline approaches and pressure rises. We just know, "There has got to be a better way."

Recently, I promised to find a solution to the frustration and wasted time caused by [*Describe problem caused by not having equipment requested, i.e., "computer," "copier," "fax machine," "printer," etc*]. Goal attainment is important to our team, and controlling the maximum number of variables is essential.

I have come up with a simple way to enhance our company's efficiency and morale. A [*Describe equipment requested, i.e., "computer," "copier," "fax machine," "printer," etc*] would accomplish this quickly. A rough cost estimate is between $[*Dollar amount of lowest estimated price of equipment requested, i.e., "computer," "copier," "fax machine," "printer," etc*] and $[*Dollar amount of highest estimated price of equipment requested, i.e., "computer," "copier," "fax machine," "printer," etc*]. Your experience may suggest a solution other than outright purchase.

We both know cost containment is an on-going [YOUR COMPANY NAME] goal. However, I believe this expense is justified. Upon receiving your authorization to procure [*Describe equipment requested, i.e., "computer," "copier," "fax machine," "printer," etc*], I will perform a thorough analysis of features, manufacturer claims, pricing, and warranty coverage. The research results will then be presented for your recommendation. Thank you in advance for your prompt decision in this matter.

cc: [COPIES TO]

Equipment Use

TO: [*First and last name of person receiving memo*]

FROM: [YOUR NAME]
[YOUR TITLE]

DATE: [DATE]

SUBJECT: Equipment Use

The right tools make our jobs easier. This holds true for everything from yardwork to professional tasks. [YOUR COMPANY NAME] gives its employees the right equipment for maximum efficiency.

When we order tools and supplies, we don't ask our employees to bear the expense. You are never charged for making a business-related call, copy, or printout, nor should you be. These are [YOUR COMPANY NAME]'s responsibilities.

All we ask in return is that you respect [YOUR COMPANY NAME] equipment as if it were your own. Handle our purchases with care. We budget very carefully to obtain the equipment you need to get the job done.

Please follow all operating instructions and observe safety precautions when using company equipment. If you see someone who is not protecting or showing respect for company property, notify [*First and last name of person responsible for handling equipment misuse*] at [*Telephone number for name of person responsible for handling equipment misuse*]. Such reports are held in the strictest confidence, so you need not fear reprisal. Thank you for your ongoing respect of company equipment. We are a team, and the equipment is for everyone to use.

cc: [COPIES TO]

Error in Insurance Claim

[DATE]

[Mr./Mrs./Ms./Dr.] [FIRST AND LAST NAME]
[TITLE]
[COMPANY]
[ADDRESS]
[CITY], [STATE] [ZIP CODE]

Reference Claim Number: [*Claim number assigned to incident by* COMPANY]

Dear [Mr./Mrs./Ms./Dr.] [LAST NAME]:

Life's best lessons are mastered during difficult and trying times. Following a calamity, only after the dust settles can a clearer picture appear. When [*Describe the event that happened covered by insurance*] on [*Date the event happened that is covered by insurance*], I tried hard throughout the initial tumultuous time to secure an accurate damage estimate.

Those efforts are now merely a good place to start. Upon careful review of the damages listing, some areas definitely require reassessment. I need your help correcting errors in our insurance claim covered under policy number [YOUR COMPANY NAME's *insurance policy number assigned by* COMPANY]. These are as follows: [*Describe and list by number the corrections*].

I regret the extra effort required to meet our expectations as a [COMPANY] client. Please know I am here to make your job easier by answering any questions that simplify prompt reimbursement.

[*First name of person receiving letter*], your professionalism then, and today, does not go unnoticed. Thank you for your assistance and understanding. Speaking for the entire team at [YOUR COMPANY NAME], I appreciate organizations that maintain high standards to sustain life-long relationships with customers.

Sincerely yours,

[YOUR NAME]
[YOUR TITLE]

Excellent Report

TO: [*First and last name of person receiving memo*]

FROM: [YOUR NAME]
[YOUR TITLE]

DATE: [DATE]

SUBJECT: Excellent Report

A good violin contains about 70 separate pieces of wood. Bit by bit, skilled designers shape the highest-sounding instrument of the modern string family. In the hands of a musician, the violin comes alive from the lowest G chord up nearly four octaves.

A review of the [*Name of the report*] report makes it clear that many pieces of supporting documentation were gathered to create a thorough presentation. Handing tools to the designer is one thing; having the work done expertly is another. From beginning to end, the report could not have had a better sound.

Thank you for expending the extra effort required to master form and content. It clearly depicts a proficiency in business skills that will enhance your future with [YOUR COMPANY NAME].

cc: [COPIES TO]

Excessive Expenses

TO: [*First and last name of person receiving memo*]

FROM: [YOUR NAME]
[YOUR TITLE]

DATE: [DATE]

SUBJECT: Controlling Expenses

Freedom is a precious gift left to businesses and individuals by our founding fathers. Their efforts laid the foundation for the American Dream that people all over the world strive to achieve. We must, however, have rules if we are to maintain order in our independent lives.

We believe that employee autonomy is crucial to [YOUR COMPANY NAME]'s success. Freedom of thought sparks creative action. Yet even when such latitude is given, we must uphold the establishment's rules.

[YOUR COMPANY NAME] has set limits on expenses to eliminate inappropriate spending. These rules, which apply to all of us, benefit the entire organization. Your recent request for reimbursement for [*Describe what the expense was for*] falls outside the area of approved expenses because it [*Describe the reason expense is excessive*].

In the future, you must get management approval prior to incurring expenses of this nature. A simple memo detailing the purpose and estimated cost must be submitted to me beforehand. My intention is not to limit your freedom within our corporation; I simply want to ensure that the rules are followed by everyone.

cc: [COPIES TO]

Excessive Sick Days

TO: [*First and last name of person receiving memo*]

FROM: [YOUR NAME]
[YOUR TITLE]

DATE: [DATE]

SUBJECT: Sick Day Discussion

Our corporate team consists of interlocking links that create the chain of accomplishment. Each link is equally important to the strength of the whole. When just one link is weak, the bond lessens and puts additional pressure on the rest.

We have empathy and understand that your recent health problems are not of your own making. Your job is an important link in our team and one that should not be underestimated. For the entire team to prosper, [YOUR COMPANY NAME] needs your resources and talents each day.

Your [*Total number of sick days taken*] absences during the past [*Time over which sick days have been taken*] fall outside the area of acceptability and place additional loads on the rest of the team. Your peers have willingly handled your duties in addition to their own. Still, this is not fair to them.

Please evaluate your present health situation and advise me in writing by [*Date by which you would like to receive name of person receiving memo's response*] of the prognosis and estimated time required for you to resume a regular work schedule. We want to help you regain your position in the team's chain. You are a valuable link.

cc: [COPIES TO]

Exchange Approval

[DATE]

[Mr./Mrs./Ms./Dr.] [CUSTOMER'S FULL NAME]
[CUSTOMER'S TITLE]
[COMPANY]
[ADDRESS]
[CITY], [STATE] [ZIP CODE]

Dear [Mr./Mrs./Ms./Dr.] [CUSTOMER'S LAST NAME]:

Because business needs do not come in shrink-wrapped boxes, every product is not exactly right for everyone. We do our best to achieve general appeal in satisfying a wide range of requirements. However, I understand that the [*Name of product purchased*] purchased from us does not meet [COMPANY]'s criteria.

After giving this situation much thought, I have concluded that a viable alternative is [*Describe the exchange offered*]. To complete the exchange, all [COMPANY] must do is [*Describe the actions necessary to perform exchange*].

I am confident you will be pleased with the exchange offered. Thank you for giving us another chance.

Sincerely yours,

[YOUR NAME]
[YOUR TITLE]

Expense Reimbursement

TO: [*First and last name of person receiving memo*]

FROM: [YOUR NAME]
[YOUR TITLE]

DATE: [DATE]

SUBJECT: Expense Reimbursement

Tight budgetary controls allow [YOUR COMPANY NAME] to operate efficiently and prudently. Successful financial management requires everyone's compliance with a few basic expense reimbursement procedures.

Submitting expenses for reimbursement is each employee's individual responsibility at [YOUR COMPANY NAME]. Expenses estimated to be more than $[*Dollar amount of expense needing prior approval*] must be approved in advance by [*First and last name of person responsible for receiving memo's expense approval*]. The procedure for expense reimbursement is as follows: [*Describe step-by-step procedure for expense reimbursement*].

Please note that expenses, with applicable invoices or receipts attached, must be received by [*First and last name of person responsible for releasing money for receiving memo's expense*] within [*Time in days by which the expense must be remitted*] days from the date incurred. Otherwise, additional approvals may be necessary prior to reimbursement. Thank you for your cooperation and assistance in maintaining respectable financial ethics.

cc: [COPIES TO]

Family Leave

TO: [*First and last name of person receiving memo*]

FROM: [YOUR NAME]
[YOUR TITLE]

DATE: [DATE]

SUBJECT: Leave of Absence Request for Family Reasons

Families cannot be replaced. Possessions and wealth lose their meaning when measured against the joy of holding a loved one's hand or welcoming a new generation into the world. To believe otherwise is to mock humanity's most basic instincts.

Being an important member of a family is a source of tremendous happiness and many responsibilities. I have been forced to make a decision recently between career and family priorities because my [*Relationship of person needing help, i.e., "brother," "child," "father," "mother," "sister," etc.*] needs my undivided attention. After exploring various solutions, I believe I am the best one to carry this burden.

The leave, if approved, would be for [*Total number of leave days requested*] days beginning on [*Date the leave begins*]. Therefore, the date of my return to work date would be [*Date the leave ends*]. I realize that this may be an inopportune time, and I will understand if you should decide not to grant my family's wish. Please advise me of your decision at your earliest convenience. Thank you for your consideration. Again, I will understand if you believe that the burden imposed by the leave would be too great for my other family, [YOUR COMPANY NAME], to bear right now.

cc: [COPIES TO]

FAX COVER SHEET

FACSIMILE COMMUNICATION
COVER SHEET

DATE: ___________

SHEET 1 OF ___________ TOTAL PAGES

TO: ______________________________________

FROM: ______________________________________

IMPORTANT NOTES:

If you do not receive complete pages or legible copy, please call [*Telephone number of your office*] immediately. The information contained in this facsimile is intended only for the use of the individual or entity named above. If you receive this fax in error, please notify us by telephone immediately at the number listed above and return the facsimile to us via First Class mail at the following address: [YOUR COMPANY NAME *address*]. We will, of course, be happy to reimburse you for the cost. Thank you.

Fire Insurance Claim

[DATE]

[Mr./Mrs./Ms./Dr.] [FIRST AND LAST NAME]
[TITLE]
[COMPANY]
[ADDRESS]
[CITY], [STATE] [ZIP CODE]

Dear [Mr./Mrs./Ms./Dr.] [LAST NAME]:

Even outstanding safety measures do not permanently protect businesses from Murphy's Law, "What can go wrong will go wrong." [YOUR COMPANY NAME] is a perfect example. At approximately [*Time fire occurred*] on [*Date fire occurred*], our company suffered a devastating tragedy. We were victims of one of life's perils and nature's wonders, a fire.

In full compliance with our [COMPANY] policy, number [YOUR COMPANY NAME's *insurance policy number assigned by* COMPANY], this damage estimate is submitted within the specified time limitations. As you might imagine, I am still gathering information. Therefore, the following represents a partial listing of the losses for [*Per insurance policy, "actual current value" or "replacement value"*] reimbursement: [*Describe and list by number damages or losses*].

I must depend on your professional advice and expertise now. Our operations cannot resume normal activity without immediate reimbursement. Insurance inherently protects investments and limits losses in unforeseen circumstances. While you may not have used those exact words, today I am glad I followed your recommendations for [YOUR COMPANY NAME]'s insurance coverage. Thank you for your assistance.

Sincerely yours,

[YOUR NAME]
[YOUR TITLE]

Flexible Work Schedule

TO: [*First and last name of person receiving memo*]

FROM: [YOUR NAME]
[YOUR TITLE]

DATE: [DATE]

SUBJECT: Flexible Work Schedule Request

Self-direction is the linchpin of achievement. Organizations count on employees to be diligent, motivated, and productive without constant reminders. Because [YOUR COMPANY NAME] is secure in allowing proven performers to use their judgment daily, I am confident that my work schedule change request will be given careful consideration.

In my role as [*Your title or position*], I am linked to [YOUR COMPANY NAME] by a function. The company has determined that my skills are best utilized to [*Describe your job in one or two words*]. My performance ratings are based on my progress toward that goal.

After much consideration, I firmly believe that [*Describe your job in one or two words*] can be accomplished under either a flexible or a traditional work schedule. I propose that my schedule be changed to reflect the following: [*Describe flexible work schedule in days and time reporting to and from work*]. These hours are equal to those I currently work.

I would like to try a flexible work schedule and recommend that the change be implemented as a temporary move. In three to six months, a situational review could be the deciding factor. Thank you in advance for your prompt consideration of my request.

cc: [COPIES TO]

Forecast Request

TO: [*First and last name of person receiving memo*]

FROM: [YOUR NAME]
[YOUR TITLE]

DATE: [DATE]

SUBJECT: Forecast Due

Marketing is what we do to obtain sales. Predicting the future is often a futile effort because so many uncertainties affect the result. Yet, making management aware of your time-based marketing and sales goals enables us to offer assistance and expertise wherever possible.

Please prepare your sales forecast for the next [*Period forecast covers*] and have it in my office by [*Date forecast is due*]. Specifically, list in chart form by customer name the following: [*Describe what you want to know*]. I am most interested in [*Describe the information most important to you*].

Please make your forecast as complete and accurate as possible. If you have any questions, contact me immediately. Contrary to popular belief, we do control our own destinies—with actions taken today.

cc: [COPIES TO]

Franchise Inquiry

[DATE]

[Mr./Mrs./Ms./Dr.] [FIRST AND LAST NAME]
[TITLE]
[COMPANY]
[ADDRESS]
[CITY], [STATE] [ZIP CODE]

Dear [Mr./Mrs./Ms./Dr.] [LAST NAME]:

Is there such a thing as a formula for success? The myriad business and consumer variables that envelop every industry have always kept me from believing so—that is, until I visited a [COMPANY] location in [*City in which you visited a* COMPANY *location*]. The operation was efficient and, at first glance, appears to be a profitable enterprise.

[YOUR COMPANY NAME] is interested in learning more about [COMPANY] with a particular curiosity about growth opportunities in [*City* YOUR COMPANY NAME *is interested in placing a* COMPANY *location*]. Please forward the following materials: [COMPANY] background, break-even analysis, estimated franchise earnings, franchisee fees, financing alternatives, approved government assistance programs, and a successful franchise's demographic profile. In addition, we are interested in obtaining [COMPANY]'s "Uniform Franchise Offering Circular." All the above can be sent to [YOUR COMPANY NAME's *address*].

I look forward to reviewing the information and discovering [COMPANY]'s formula for franchise success. Thank you in advance for your reply. [YOUR COMPANY NAME] would like to share in your breakthrough.

Sincerely yours,

[YOUR NAME]
[YOUR TITLE]

Freelance Work Agreement

RECITALS:

This is [YOUR COMPANY NAME]'s standard agreement to confirm a freelance work arrangement where we are referred to as "Customer"and [COMPANY] is the "Contractor."

FREELANCE WORK AGREEMENT

Customer hereby requests Contractor to prepare the following: Description of Work: [*Describe and list by number work performed by* COMPANY] Date Due: [*Date work performed by* COMPANY *is due*]

Customer agrees to pay Contractor $[*Cost of and list by number work to be performed by* COMPANY] upon timely receipt and acceptance of the work. All work done under this Freelance Work Agreement is considered "work for hire,"meaning that Contractor is not an employee of Customer, and Contractor is solely responsible for any and all taxes (state, federal, and local), worker's compensation insurance payments, disability payments, social security payments, unemployment insurance payments, other insurance payments, and any similar type of payment for Contractor or employee thereof. Contractor warrants the work is an original work that has not been previously created and is free of any unauthorized derivations from other sources. Customer retains the right to refer to Contractor in any advertising or promotional material.

Please acknowledge your acceptance of this Freelance Work Agreement by completing the areas below, and return one copy to my attention. Thank you in advance for your assistance.

____

[YOUR NAME]
[YOUR TITLE]

I, [*First and last name of* COMPANY's *representative*] on behalf of [COMPANY], agree to perform the work indicated above under the terms and conditions of this Freelance Work Agreement.

____

Signature and Date

____

Social Security Number

Good Job

TO: [*First and last name of person receiving memo*]

FROM: [YOUR NAME]
[YOUR TITLE]

DATE: [DATE]

SUBJECT: Outstanding Performance

"Citius, Altius, Fortius!" This Latin phrase is the Olympic motto, meaning in modern English, "Swifter, Higher, Stronger!" Every four years, athletes from around the globe meet with this phrase ringing in their ears.

Winners need internal fortitude. The desire for success must drown out any thought of failure. Your performance on [*Reason for the recognition*] truly deserves the gold medal.

In going beyond the call of duty, you displayed the most admirable of professional attributes. It is [YOUR COMPANY NAME]'s pleasure to have you on our Olympic team. Thank you for being a role model, for proving that success is there for the taking when desire is strong.

cc: [COPIES TO]

Grand Opening

[DATE]

[Mr./Mrs./Ms./Dr.] [CUSTOMER'S FULL NAME]
[CUSTOMER'S TITLE]
[COMPANY]
[ADDRESS]
[CITY], [STATE] [ZIP CODE]

Dear [Mr./Mrs./Ms./Dr.] [CUSTOMER'S LAST NAME]:

I looked at the calendar recently and thought, "Has it been that long?" For what seems like both a minute and year, we have been working toward this special day. Visions changed quickly, and now the grand opening of [YOUR COMPANY NAME]'s [*Describe what is being opened, i.e., "new offices," "another location," or "remodeled store"*] is a reality.

We extend this personal invitation to a special few. Please join our celebration on [*Date of grand opening*] from [*Time grand opening begins*] to [*Time grand opening ends*] at [*Location of grand opening*]. It's our way of thanking our clients and friends for their encouragement and support. If for only five minutes, please stop by and allow the entire family of [YOUR COMPANY NAME] professionals to express our appreciation in person. It would be our honor.

Sincerely yours,

[YOUR NAME]
[YOUR TITLE]

Have Not Received Response

[DATE]

[Mr./Mrs./Ms./Dr.] [CUSTOMER'S FULL NAME]
[CUSTOMER'S TITLE]
[COMPANY]
[ADDRESS]
[CITY], [STATE] [ZIP CODE]

Dear [Mr./Mrs./Ms./Dr.] [CUSTOMER'S LAST NAME]:

We form relationships gradually. One action alone does not create an enduring business affiliation. [COMPANY] has waited long enough for [YOUR COMPANY NAME] to prove that no competition surpasses us.

Perhaps our contract is in that pile of things you have been meaning to do. Certainly, we all get overwhelmed at times. We need your help, though, before [YOUR COMPANY NAME] can move forward with our plan to improve [COMPANY]'s operations.

The contracts for [*Describe what the contract is for*] are necessary to our business. Thank you in advance for the speedy return of the signed contract. I am eager to turn those words into actions that will further strengthen our business relationship.

Sincerely yours,

[YOUR NAME]
[YOUR TITLE]

Hiring of Relatives

TO: All Staff

FROM: [YOUR NAME]
[YOUR TITLE]

DATE: [DATE]

SUBJECT: Hiring of Relatives

Family members are often among our most treasured friends. [YOUR COMPANY NAME] is honored when employees' family members want to join our team of professionals. The confidence shown in these referrals confirms our belief that [YOUR COMPANY NAME] is a good place to work.

However, relatives may cause conflicts due to the natural tendency toward favoritism. In addition, we run the risk of having personal problems brought into the workplace. Either of these scenarios could have a detrimental effect on employee morale.

Still, we encourage the hiring of relatives when a reporting or direct relationship will not occur. Of course, relatives are not given any special consideration in the application and hiring process. All applicants are treated equally and must meet the same set of criteria when they apply for employment with [YOUR COMPANY NAME].

[*First and last name of person responsible in human resources or personnel*] can answer any questions you may have pertaining to the hiring of relatives. We appreciate your continuous efforts to bring the most qualified employees to our team.

cc: [COPIES TO]

Hiring the Agency

[DATE]

[Mr./Mrs./Ms./Dr.] [FIRST AND LAST NAME]
[TITLE]
[COMPANY]
[ADDRESS]
[CITY], [STATE] [ZIP CODE]

Dear [Mr./Mrs./Ms./Dr.] [LAST NAME]:

Today, more than ever, transactions speak in the loudest voice. After careful review, [YOUR COMPANY NAME] has decided that your firm is best equipped to help us achieve our advertising goals. The campaign [COMPANY] presented was excellent, and our entire management team is excited by its profit potential.

Due to the nature of our business, [YOUR COMPANY NAME] requires final approval of all media placements before publication. Do call upon me for comments and suggestions during the idea-to-print process. Should [COMPANY] receive any sales inquiries during the term of our contract, please refer them to [*First and last name of* YOUR COMPANY NAME's *contact for sales inquiries*].

Let's talk soon, as there are still contracts to sign and financial arrangements to solidify. I look forward to a long and rewarding relationship and extend a big "Congratulations!"for winning [YOUR COMPANY NAME]'s account.

Sincerely yours,

[YOUR NAME]
[YOUR TITLE]

Ill Employee

TO: [*First and last name of person receiving memo*]

FROM: [YOUR NAME]'
[YOUR TITLE]

DATE: [DATE]

SUBJECT: [*First and last name of person ill*]'s Health and Our Support

Who among us has not heard that giving to others in time of need is mankind's responsibility? Neither art nor science can possibly replace the understanding human heart and touch. When a comrade falls ill, fellowship helps keep his or her face turned toward sunshine instead clouds.

As many know, our friend and co-worker, [*First and last name of person ill*], has been taken ill and will require a lengthy recuperation period. It is our individual responsibility to let [*First name of person ill*] know we care about [*Pronoun referring to gender, i.e., "his" or "her"*] welfare. While we cannot prescribe a magical cure, there is one important thing each of us can do as our share of the healing process.

A moment is all it takes to extend compassion, whether through a card, a telephone call, a basket of flowers, or a home-cooked meal. Take time from your busy schedule today to do something for [*First name of person ill*]. There are inevitable rewards in unselfish actions.

cc: [COPIES TO]

Immediate Shipment Request

[DATE]

[Mr./Mrs./Ms./Dr.] [FIRST AND LAST NAME]
[TITLE]
[COMPANY]
[ADDRESS]
[CITY], [STATE] [ZIP CODE]

Dear [Mr./Mrs./Ms./Dr.] [LAST NAME]:

The word "watch" originated in England when town watchmen were common sights. These watchmen, who walked through town crying out the hour, were among the first to carry portable timepieces. Glancing at my date- and time-equipped 21st century watch in a recent staff meeting, I became aware of a situation requiring [COMPANY]'s assistance.

Under normal conditions, I would not ask for special arrangements in order delivery. Circumstances beyond my control, however, demand that [*Name of product*], ordered on [*Date name of product was ordered*], be in our possession no later than the close of business on [*Date is required*].

Before shipment, please obtain my approval on any additional [COMPANY] charges required to accommodate our request. My clock is ticking, and pressures are mounting. I look forward to receiving confirmation that our request is being handled. Your professional assistance in ensuring delivery within these time limitations is greatly appreciated.

Sincerely yours,

[YOUR NAME]
[YOUR TITLE]

Improved Performance

TO: [*First and last name of person receiving memo*]

FROM: [YOUR NAME]
[YOUR TITLE]

DATE: [DATE]

SUBJECT: Improved Performance

The wise person sees constructive criticism as a way to tap into another's experience to better his or her own. Taking advice and putting it into action is a true test of character. We must trust, however, that the person making the recommendations has our best interest in mind.

I am pleased that you welcomed my appraisal of [*Problem brought to first and last name of person receiving memo's attention*] and did not perceive it as a personal or professional attack. You took the initiative and action that resulted in positive growth. Most important, your improvement reflects the commitment I believe you have to yourself, our team, and [YOUR COMPANY NAME]. [*First name of of person receiving memo*], thank you for making the recommended changes and for your continuing support of our business practices.

cc: [COPIES TO]

Improvement Plan

TO: [*First and last name of person receiving memo*]

FROM: [YOUR NAME]
[YOUR TITLE]

DATE: [DATE]

SUBJECT: Performance Improvement Plan

It takes confidence and intelligence to embrace constructive criticism as a beneficial recommendation rather than a personal attack. When we fail to meet company expectations, recommendations help us change our behavior and get back on the road to success. Having the finest team members is important to [YOUR COMPANY NAME].

Each day should be marked with another advancement toward our personal and professional pinnacles of success. I am happy to be a mentor to people who have the ability to accomplish great things.

As your mentor, I must tell you candidly that the probability of success is not very high for you right now. Your performance is being restricted by the following: [*Describe areas requiring improvement*]

I believe that your attention and commitment to changing the above inadequacies will bring about an immediate improvement. We will monitor your progress over the next [*Time your company policy allots for improvement plans*] to determine whether any further action is necessary. Please do not disappoint us. The way you respond will have a lasting effect on your career.

cc: [COPIES TO]

In the Media

TO: [*First and last name of person receiving memo*]

FROM: [YOUR NAME]
[YOUR TITLE]

DATE: [DATE]

SUBJECT: [YOUR COMPANY NAME] in the Media

Since the late 1950s, quiz shows have provided high ratings for television producers and networks. Starting with CBS-TV's $64,000 Question, hundreds of contestant-oriented shows promising big dollars for the right answers have worked their way into America's homes. ABC-TV had Twenty-One, and The $64,000 Question had a brother, The $64,000 Challenge.

After Charles Van Doren, a Columbia University professor and member of the acclaimed literary Van Doren family, won $129,000 over six weeks, a scandal broke. Newspapers ran an exposé that the shows were rigged. Contestants were coached on the right answers and how to fake dramatics while puzzling out the correct response.

While television learned a valuable lesson, so did the media. Scandals sell newspapers. Newspaper sales stimulate advertising sales. Advertising sales increase profits. The vicious cycle continues, and today we are the subject of the hype created by the media. Unlike those quiz shows, we have nothing to hide. Our comments and position on [*Subject of media coverage*] are forthright and accurate.

Information was taken out of context and interpreted in a way that gave the media what they wanted in the first place—increased sales. There is always a victim in these situations. In the quiz show scandal, many innocent people lost their jobs. Be assured that we are taking all steps necessary to rectify this situation and maintain the fine reputation of our corporation and its employees. We have nothing to hide, and we appreciate your support.

cc: [COPIES TO]

Inactive Customer Questionnaire

[DATE]

[Mr./Mrs./Ms./Dr.] [CUSTOMER'S FULL NAME]
[CUSTOMER'S TITLE]
[COMPANY]
[ADDRESS]
[CITY], [STATE] [ZIP CODE]

Dear [Mr./Mrs./Ms./Dr.] [CUSTOMER'S LAST NAME]:

You probably thought that we had forgotten about you, that your business could not be all that important to a big company like [YOUR COMPANY NAME]. I have news for you; you and your business are important to us. There must be a good reason to explain why [COMPANY] has not purchased from us for some time.

I work hard at customer relationships, and when one ends, I take it personally. I know I shouldn't, but I can't help it. Would you please take a moment to answer a few questions?

1. What is the main reason you haven't ordered from us?

   ____

2. What could we have done differently in handling your account?

   ____

3. On a scale of 1 to 10, where 1 is the lowest possible score and 10 the highest, please rate the following:
   The courtesy and knowledge of our staff. _____
   The overall customer service efforts. _____
   The competitive pricing of our products _____
   The quality of our operations. _____
4. What can we do to welcome you back as our customer?

   ____

Just drop this letter in the mail using the enclosed self-addressed, stamped envelope. You have my promise that your answers will be held in strictest confidence. Thank you for your time. Your ideas and responses will help us learn how to serve you better.

Sincerely yours,

[YOUR NAME]
[YOUR TITLE]

Incomplete Information

[DATE]

[Mr./Mrs./Ms./Dr.] [CUSTOMER'S FULL NAME]
[CUSTOMER'S TITLE]
[COMPANY]
[ADDRESS]
[CITY], [STATE] [ZIP CODE]

Dear [Mr./Mrs./Ms./Dr.] [CUSTOMER'S LAST NAME]:

Imagine getting absorbed in an action-packed novel only to discover that it was missing a few chapters? The story would lack the continuity and flow needed to create an engaging plot. [YOUR COMPANY NAME]'s order form does not lend much creativity, but it does provide the whole story.

[COMPANY]'s order placed on [*Date order was placed*] for [*Describe what the order was for*] is missing a few character sketches. Specifically, we need to know [*Describe the information needed to complete order*].

For your convenience, just [*Manner in which the information can be sent to* YOUR COMPANY NAME, *i.e., "fax," "mail," or "telephone"*] the information to our order department. We want to have the required materials in your hands as soon as possible. Only then will every chapter be complete, allowing us to reach the end of this story and start a new one.

Sincerely yours,

Increasing Cost of Benefits

TO: [*First and last name of person receiving memo*]

FROM: [YOUR NAME]
[YOUR TITLE]

DATE: [DATE]

SUBJECT: Benefits Costs Increasing

During these inflationary times, it's hard to believe that ten cents once bought a loaf of bread or made a telephone call. Times have certainly changed, and so has the price of health care. Until health care reform becomes more than a political promise, consumers will have to bear the burden.

Unfortunately, we have been notified that [*Name of health care provider*] has increased its premiums by [*Amount of the increase in percent*] percent effective [*Date the price increase takes effect*]. [YOUR COMPANY NAME] is dedicated to providing a comprehensive benefits program for our employees. Upon hearing the news, management requested an examination of the premium increase.

Health care costs have increased across the board; there was nothing we could do. However, [*Name of health care provider*] is still quite competitive in the health care marketplace, offering a comprehensive, cost-effective plan. There is one thing you can do. Write to your representatives in Congress and let them know how increases in health care costs have affected your life. Like a vote, one voice does make a difference.

cc: [COPIES TO]

Interest in Possible Acquisition

[DATE]

[Mr./Mrs./Ms./Dr.] [FIRST AND LAST NAME]
[TITLE]
[COMPANY]
[ADDRESS]
[CITY], [STATE] [ZIP CODE]

Dear [Mr./Mrs./Ms./Dr.] [LAST NAME]:

Studying the past often reveals truths for today. The classic 17th century text on Japanese warfare by Miyamoto Musashi, *A Book of Five Rings*, contains valuable insight for both samurai warriors and business professionals. The pages of winning moves have taught me many lessons over the years.

While open to interpretation, one of the things I have learned is that achievers need to "see distant things as if they were close." I congratulate you on successfully creating in [COMPANY] a dominant force in the [*Describe* COMPANY's *main business emphasis*] industry. It took a great deal of hard work and vision to achieve such stature.

Because of this, [YOUR COMPANY NAME] is interested in learning more about [COMPANY] with a specific goal. Our staff has identified your company from a distance as one that we might be interested in acquiring. If this looks like a winning move for you and [COMPANY], please assume a proactive stance by telephoning me at your convenience. I look forward to future discussions with you and your associates.

Sincerely yours,

[YOUR NAME]
[YOUR TITLE]

Invoice Error

[DATE]

[Mr./Mrs./Ms./Dr.] [CUSTOMER'S FULL NAME]
[CUSTOMER'S TITLE]
[COMPANY]
[ADDRESS]
[CITY], [STATE] [ZIP CODE]

Dear [Mr./ Mrs./Ms./Dr.] [CUSTOMER'S LAST NAME]:

A company that catches its errors is just about as perfect as a company can be. Even [YOUR COMPANY NAME]'s commitment to total quality management has not made us faultless. Our routine checks found an error in the invoice for [COMPANY]'s recent purchase of [*Describe purchase(s) invoice represents*].

The [*Describe the place where error is on invoice*] on invoice number [*Number on invoice used for tracking purposes*] should have been [*Describe the correction for error on invoice*], not [*Describe the error in detail*]. To correct this mistake, we ask you to call [*First and last name of* YOUR COMPANY NAME's *credit representative*] at the earliest convenience. Thank you for your patience and cooperation in this matter. No one can declare perfection in every arena; we can only continue to strive for it. The only things that [YOUR COMPANY NAME] can guarantee are honesty and customer satisfaction.

Sincerely yours,

[YOUR NAME]
[YOUR TITLE]

Job Offer Confirmation

TO: [*First and last name of person receiving memo*]

FROM: [YOUR NAME]
[YOUR TITLE]

DATE: [DATE]

SUBJECT: Job Offer Confirmation for [*First and last name of person to be hired*]

Developing a highly effective team is an enduring goal for successful companies like [YOUR COMPANY NAME]. We must strive to integrate only the most knowledgeable, skilled, and talented players into our operation. Clearly, your endorsement of [*First and last name of person to be hired*] as a [*Title of position person to be hired will assume*] speaks loudly regarding [*Pronoun referring to person to be hired's gender, i.e., "his" or "her"*] abilities as a team player.

I have reviewed [*First and last name of person to be hired]*'s resume and application for employment along with notes from our conversations. We agree that [YOUR COMPANY NAME] would benefit from [*Pronoun referring to person to be hired's gender, i.e., "his" or "her"*] background and experience. Based upon competitive market salary data, we are prepared to offer [*First and last name of person to be hired*] $[*Dollar amount based on "hour," "month," or year to be paid*] per [*Period salary is based on, i.e., "hour," "month," or year*].

Please provide this information to the candidate in writing as soon as possible and advise me when you expect to bring [*First and last name of person to be hired*] on board. Thank you for your assistance in selecting our newest team member.

cc: [COPIES TO]

Jury Duty Excuse

[DATE]

[Mr./Mrs./Ms./Dr.] [FIRST AND LAST NAME]
[TITLE]
[COMPANY]
[ADDRESS]
[CITY], [STATE] [ZIP CODE]

Dear [Mr./Mrs./Ms./Dr.] [LAST NAME]:

It is truly an honor to be an American and live in this great nation. Respecting equality, freedom, and justice is every society member's responsibility. Through jury duty, the judicial system promotes appreciation of these ideals.

Far too many voices cry that laws and legislation are administered without regard for public opinion. Jury duty is a small price to pay for the benefits of United States citizenship. However, we regret that, due to circumstances beyond [YOUR COMPANY NAME]'s control, [*First and last name of employee*] will be unable to report for jury duty on the date stated in [*Pronoun referring to employee's gender, i.e., "his" or "her"*] summons.

Please know I have taken a personal interest in changing the situation that prevents [*First and last name of employee*] from fulfilling [*Pronoun referring to employee's gender, i.e., "his" or "her"*] responsibility. Under different circumstances, there would be no question of [*First and last name of employee*]'s participation. Thank you for your understanding in the matter. As a law abiding company, we do wish things had been different.

Sincerely yours,

[YOUR NAME]
[YOUR TITLE]

Late Payment Apology

[DATE]

[Mr./Mrs./Ms./Dr.] [FIRST AND LAST NAME]
[TITLE]
[COMPANY]
[ADDRESS]
[CITY], [STATE] [ZIP CODE]

Dear [Mr./Mrs./Ms./Dr.] [LAST NAME]:

Poor business practices are remembered longer than respectable habits. I recently was informed by my staff that a potential mark may have been placed on [YOUR COMPANY NAME]'s character. While our account remittance policies are normally followed diligently, the paperwork authorizing payment to [COMPANY] was subject to pure negligence, and my staff has been reprimanded.

I have enclosed $[*Dollar amount of payment made with the enclosed check*], check number [*Number on* YOUR COMPANY NAME *check*], for invoice number [*Invoice number issued by* COMPANY *for payment*]. Our balance after posting this payment is [*Balance on* YOUR COMPANY NAME *account with* COMPANY].

[YOUR COMPANY NAME] is very much like [COMPANY] in many ways. We both appreciate prompt payment, if for no other reason than to keep the books under control. I extend my apology with sincere regret and thank you for your patience. Let's return to business as usual and put this embarrassing blunder behind us.

Sincerely yours,

[YOUR NAME]
[YOUR TITLE]

Late Report Apology

TO: [*First and last name of person receiving memo*]

FROM: [YOUR NAME]
[YOUR TITLE]

DATE: [DATE]

SUBJECT: Apology

Perfectionism is both a blessing and a curse. My desire for excellence has uncovered areas in the [*Name of project, report, or task*] report that require additional effort and research. Rather than submitting a report that fails to meet our standards, I intend to continue to devote extra energy to ensuring the information's accuracy and validity.

These steps will require that I spend more time on the task. However, I will do my very best to have the complete [*Name of project, report, or task*] report in your hands no later than [*Date by which you will provide report*]. Please accept my apologies for any inconvenience this delay has caused.

cc: [COPIES TO]

Lateness on Hours

TO: [*First and last name of person receiving memo*]

FROM: [YOUR NAME]
[YOUR TITLE]

DATE: [DATE]

SUBJECT: Dependability

Principles are the backbone of success. Whether we strive for financial gain or a happy family life, the ethical ground upon which we stand serves as the ultimate foundation. People can give us advice, but we determine our own destinies.

We hear the words confidence, integrity, and respect quite often in life. Professionally, one behavior that impairs our relationships with our co-workers and customers is tardiness.

Frankly, tardiness reflects a lack of concern. Being late tells those who are waiting for you that you don't care enough about them or their time to make the effort needed to be on time. For your professional growth, promptness is a necessary habit.

Setting your watch a few minutes fast works. Some people require only a gentle reminder. Thank you for devoting the necessary energy to acquiring this very important professional attribute. The best way to learn promptness is through practice.

cc: [COPIES TO]

Lawyer's Review

[DATE]

[Mr./Mrs./Ms./Dr.] [FIRST AND LAST NAME]
[TITLE]
[COMPANY]
[ADDRESS]
[CITY], [STATE] [ZIP CODE]

Dear [Mr./Mrs./Ms./Dr.] [LAST NAME]:

Laws are intended to promote good conduct and minimize contempt. Written by people to serve people, governing principles are subject to interpretation. As expected, agreements generated by one company for another's signature are tainted with obvious bias.

This is why I forward the agreement drafted by [*Name of* COMPANY *that provided legal agreement*] for your analysis and review. The agreement serves to solidify the terms and conditions of [YOUR COMPANY NAME]'s relationship with [*Name of* COMPANY *that provided legal agreement*] to [*Describe and list by number purposes of agreement*]. My primary concern with the agreement as it stands is [*Describe your main concern in agreement*].

Before you start, I would appreciate some idea of how many hours you expect to spend reviewing the agreement and an anticipated completion date. Should you have any questions or require supporting documentation, let me know. Thank you for your assistance. Your expertise guarantees that our present and future interests will be protected.

Sincerely yours,

[YOUR NAME]
[YOUR TITLE]

Layoffs

TO: [*First and last name of person receiving memo*]

FROM: [YOUR NAME]
[YOUR TITLE]

DATE: [DATE]

SUBJECT: Reduction in Work Force

Like our climate, businesses have seasons. We emerge in the spring, celebrate in summer, shed in the fall, and hibernate in winter. And we plant seeds throughout the year to assure growth. However, a single storm can destroy the farmer's harvest. Left are difficult decisions affecting many families.

Directional changes occur during economically challenging times when the crop exceeds the demand. Operations must be streamlined, work forces reduced. Unfortunately, our organization is faced with hardships that require us to make drastic changes if we are to maintain our market presence.

It is with utmost regret that I inform our corporate family that there is no way of returning to springtime favor without a work force reduction. Following extensive analysis and review, we have decided to lay off personnel in the [*Name of the department, division, job title, etc affected by layoff*]. Those directly affected will be advised by their managers on [*Date the people let go will be notified*].

This loss places an additional burden of performance on each of us. We are asking all of you to carry more than your share of the load until the seedlings of corporate development have had a chance to take root. Only then will we be able to reap the rewards of a bountiful crop.

cc: [COPIES TO]

Layoff Due to Change

TO: [*First and last name of person receiving memo*]

FROM: [YOUR NAME]
[YOUR TITLE]

DATE: [DATE]

SUBJECT: Business Changes Require Layoffs

There is no good way to tell someone bad news. Inevitably, shock and despair set in no matter how hard one tries to soften the blow. With this in mind, please know that I have taken all steps necessary on your behalf to attempt to change the situation.

[YOUR COMPANY NAME]'s business direction and profits have undergone significant changes. This requires a refocusing of resources that is imperative for survival. To regain our market placement, we must cut expenses immediately throughout the organization. I regret to inform you that effective [*Date person receiving memo will be laid off*], we will no longer require your skills. [*First and last name of person responsible for handling layoff details*] will be contacting you shortly with the layoff details and termination package.

Please be assured that I would change this unfortunate situation if I had the authority and the opportunity. You have been a valuable addition to our company, and you will be missed. I am concerned about your welfare; let me know if we can help. I have always considered you more than an employee; I consider you a valuable team player. It will be my pleasure to provide references to your prospective employers.

cc: [COPIES TO]

Lead Sharing Agreement

[DATE]

[Mr./Mrs./Ms./Dr.] [FIRST AND LAST NAME]
[TITLE]
[COMPANY]
[ADDRESS]
[CITY], [STATE] [ZIP CODE]

Dear [Mr./Mrs./Ms./Dr.] [LAST NAME]:

Many professionals wrongly believe marketing tactics are the same as marketing strategies. Although interrelated, the two are distinct. Tactics are the techniques used by corporate armies to secure the strategy's goals.

[YOUR COMPANY NAME] implemented this distinction throughout the ranks long ago. One of our tactics is to join forces with allies to win customer support. [COMPANY]'s name was brought to my attention by our staff as the leader in the [*Describe* COMPANY's *main business emphasis*] industry.

Clearly, we are not competitors, as our primary focus is [*Describe* YOUR COMPANY NAME's *main business emphasis*]. A collaboration through lead sharing would enhance both of our businesses. The many ways to achieve this goal warrant a meeting on the subject. If you are interested in pursuing this tactic, please telephone me to explore the implementation of a lead-sharing program. I look forward to exploring with you a mutually beneficial relationship.

Sincerely yours,

[YOUR NAME]
[YOUR TITLE]

Make Decision

[DATE]

[Mr./Mrs./Ms./Dr.] [CUSTOMER'S FULL NAME]
[CUSTOMER'S TITLE]
[COMPANY]
[ADDRESS]
[CITY], [STATE] [ZIP CODE]

Dear [Mr./Mrs./Ms./Dr.] [CUSTOMER'S LAST NAME]:

Franz Schubert's masterpiece, his Sixth Symphony, was rejected by the Paris Symphony Orchestra. The London Philharmonic laughed. The piece was not played in public until 30 years after it was written. Now experts consider Schubert's Sixth Symphony one of the greatest works of all time.

While things have undoubtedly changed since Schubert's day, it still takes time to gain confidence and trust in business relationships. Yet, [YOUR COMPANY NAME] can't sing our song without your decision to serve as the ultimate conductor of our moves.

Our company's symphony has many parts, and the best critics are applauding the high-quality [*Describe* YOUR COMPANY NAME's *main business emphasis and what you are trying to market to* COMPANY] they receive. Don't let another moment pass; let's get started. [YOUR COMPANY NAME] is a masterpiece hidden in the sea of merchants. Call me and make today a turning point in your company's future.

Sincerely yours,

[YOUR NAME]
[YOUR TITLE]

Manager Promoted

TO: [*First and last name of person receiving memo*]

FROM: [YOUR NAME]
[YOUR TITLE]

DATE: [DATE]

SUBJECT: Your Achievement Recognition

Management principles are ubiquitous. Many believe that the formula for effective management consists of using the right words—"increased productivity"and "team spirit," for example. While good managers may speak the same language, there are often differences in the way they speak that language.

Accenting the syllables properly is one of the keys to success. As my manager, you always used pitches and tones that were pleasing to my ears and spurred me on in my career with [YOUR COMPANY NAME]. It appears now that others more important than I have recognized your management skills as well.

Congratulations on your well-deserved promotion to [*Title of promotion*]. I could not do justice to a list of all you have given me personally and professionally. Let me just say thank you for being a good, effective manager and facilitating the development of my skills.

cc: [COPIES TO]

Manager Support

TO: [*First and last name of person receiving memo*]

FROM: [YOUR NAME]
[YOUR TITLE]

DATE: [DATE]

SUBJECT: Thank You

I have often wondered whether goal attainment is encouraged more by managerial support in and of itself or the confidence engendered by that support. Your actions regarding [*Describe the most recent job, project, or task person receiving this memo helped you with*] clearly lend credence to both hypotheses.

The extra effort, patience, and time you willingly dedicate to ensuring the accuracy and completeness of my work do not go unnoticed. My experience with other managers gives me an even greater appreciation of you.

[*First name off person receiving memo*], thank you for giving me the confidence I need to excel in my life. It means even more coming from a person of your stature.

cc: [COPIES TO]

Maternity Absence Request

TO: [*First and last name of person receiving memo*]

FROM: [YOUR NAME]
[YOUR TITLE]

DATE: [DATE]

SUBJECT: Leave of Absence Request for Maternity Reasons

For many of us, the ultimate gift is the feeling we get when looking into a small child's eyes. Somewhere in that sparkle, there is a little part of you and your heritage, and there will be so much for the child to see as life unfolds. Birth is nothing less than a miracle.

Amid the exciting preparations, my professional career aspirations have become stronger than ever. Like my parents and their parents, I want my child to have nothing but the best experiences and opportunities.

I am requesting a maternity leave that, barring any unforeseen circumstances, will last from [*Date the leave begins*] through [*Date the leave ends*]. This bonding period is necessary for our family. In addition, plans must be made to assimilate an infant's needs gracefully into our professional lives.

You have my home telephone number; please feel free to call with even the smallest question. I look forward to sharing this gift of life with my [YOUR COMPANY NAME] family. If not in person, I promise to bring in my share of those "Look at my beautiful baby" pictures.

cc: [COPIES TO]

Medical Leave Request

TO: [*First and last name of person receiving memo*]

FROM: [YOUR NAME]
[YOUR TITLE]

DATE: [DATE]

SUBJECT: Leave of Absence Request for Medical Reasons

In our day-to-day existence, we tend to take things for granted unless something out of the ordinary forces us to sit up and take notice. The car that starts in the morning and the copy machine that works are just two examples. Until now, I had never given much thought to what I would do if for some reason my health was temporarily taken from me.

The right food, proper exercise, and an active mind has served me well over the years. Today, however, I find myself in a precarious position. Despite my desire to continue doing my job with all the dedication and energy I normally put forth, health limitations have made it impossible for me to do so.

My friends and physicians tell me I am pushing the healing process, which invariably does the opposite and lengthens the cycle. Therefore, for our mutual benefit, I would like to take a medical leave of absence from [*Date the leave begins*] through [*Date the leave ends*].

I expect my health problem caused by [*Health reason for leave*] to be completely under control before returning to work with renewed vitality. Thank you for understanding that this leave is necessary for [YOUR COMPANY NAME] to have this team player back in full force.

cc: [COPIES TO]

Meeting Recap

[DATE]

[Mr./Mrs./Ms./Dr.] [CUSTOMER'S FULL NAME]
[CUSTOMER'S TITLE]
[COMPANY]
[ADDRESS]
[CITY], [STATE] [ZIP CODE]

Dear [Mr./Mrs./Ms./Dr.] [CUSTOMER'S LAST NAME]:

My adrenaline pumps when I do a job well. Thank you for sharing your time at the meeting regarding [*Describe the subject of the meeting*]. We accomplished a great deal, and I look forward to moving ahead with the knowledge gleaned.

Although I envision a clear path, a few immediate steps must be taken first. I am planning to [*Describe your next actions as they relate to the meeting*]. Your participation in the project is essential, so I hope you don't mind if I keep you advised of any developments. Again, I express my thanks for the opportunity to work with you in making my professional career more fulfilling. I'm in business to help your business succeed.

Sincerely yours,

[YOUR NAME]
[YOUR TITLE]

Meeting Confirmation

TO: [*First and last name of person receiving memo*]

FROM: [YOUR NAME]
[YOUR TITLE]

DATE: [DATE]

SUBJECT: [*One or two words defining meeting*] Meeting Confirmation

Once upon a time, a plain ol' wall calendar did the trick just fine. Nowadays, we rely on more sophisticated tools as we plan our days. First we embraced notebook-sized, then pocket, and now electronic calendar systems to help us organize our lives.

Please check whatever tool you use to track appointments and be sure that our meeting about [*One or two words defining meeting*] is scheduled. As a quick confirmation, we are gathering at [*Time the meeting begins*] in [*Place within office where meeting will be held*]. I don't think the meeting will last much longer than [*Estimated duration of meeting*]. This should provide enough time to cover the issues and new developments since we last discussed [*One or two words defining meeting*].

cc: [COPIES TO]

Merger

TO: All Staff

FROM: [YOUR NAME]
[YOUR TITLE]

DATE: [DATE]

SUBJECT: Combining Companies for Maximum Reach

Throughout history, advancements have been attributed to the vision of individuals looking beyond what the consensus deemed acceptable. Futurists saw a need for change, set goals in their minds, and ignored the bantering and negative opinions of others. Whether exploring uncharted territory or finding a cure for a devastating disease, great men and women have always embraced change and recognized potential.

Foresight has enabled [YOUR COMPANY NAME] to accomplish our goal of being a strong company equipped for long-term growth. As market conditions become more competitive and economically driven, this vision must be realigned. [YOUR COMPANY NAME] has determined that our goals will be best met by combining resources with the well-respected [*Name of organization being merged with* YOUR COMPANY NAME].

For the merger to be successful, we must work together. I ask each of you to promise one thing. That is, challenge yourself to move out of your comfort zone and welcome this change as an opportunity. A bit of initial uncertainty is unavoidable. Be strong and stand by our company in creating the greatest opportunity of all time. You have my promise that the new territory we are about to explore is full of prosperity.

cc: [COPIES TO]

Merger/Acquisition Announcement

[DATE]

[Mr./Mrs./Ms./Dr.] [CUSTOMER'S FULL NAME]
[CUSTOMER'S TITLE]
[COMPANY]
[ADDRESS]
[CITY], [STATE] [ZIP CODE]

Dear [Mr./Mrs./Ms./Dr.] [CUSTOMER'S LAST NAME]:

Survival in this business-driven and time-oriented world requires a proactive competitive stance. Reactive moves are often too late and can result in losses. Taking the initiative, [YOUR COMPANY NAME] has found a perfect complement to our company. Joining forces with this company is destined to benefit operations and, more important, our customers.

[*Name of* COMPANY *merged with or bought by* YOUR COMPANY NAME] has been in the [*Name of* COMPANY *merged with or bought by* YOUR COMPANY NAME's *industry segment*] business for some time now, and we believe that the combination of our companies will enable us to exceed market demands. This move does change our relationship for the better.

The additional products and support offered by [*Name of* COMPANY *merged with or bought by* YOUR COMPANY NAME] are the answer to all [COMPANY]'s [*Describe the main products sold by* YOUR COMPANY NAME *and Name of* COMPANY *merged with or bought by* YOUR COMPANY NAME] needs. Should you require information or just have a question, please do not hesitate to call. I am here whenever you need me.

Sincerely yours,

[YOUR NAME]
[YOUR TITLE]

Misrepresentation by Salesperson

[DATE]

[Mr./Mrs./Ms./Dr.] [FIRST AND LAST NAME]
[TITLE]
[COMPANY]
[ADDRESS]
[CITY], [STATE] [ZIP CODE]

Dear [Mr./Mrs./Ms./Dr.] [LAST NAME]:

Business transactions may be ruled by contracts, but customers still need a certain amount of faith and trust. Employees, from the chairman of the board straight down the organizational chart, act as agents and voices representing the company. However, I have learned to expect a little puff-speak from a company's marketing staff.

I deal with many sales professionals regularly. [*First and last name of* COMPANY *salesperson*] from [COMPANY] was not the first to walk through our doors. Stretching the truth and telling a complete lie to close a sale are one in the same to me. [*First and last name of* COMPANY *salesperson*] did a lot of both, and I authorized the purchase of [*Product name of what* COMPANY *salesperson sold you*] under the assumption it was [*Describe and list by number salesperson's misrepresentations*].

Today, our company suffers the effects of trusting [COMPANY]. [*First and last name of* COMPANY *salesperson*]'s statements were not accurate. I suggest you take immediate action. [YOUR COMPANY NAME] will not consider silencing this misrepresentation of the facts even with an immediate full refund in the amount of $[*Dollar amount of price paid for item(s) misrepresented by* COMPANY *salesperson's misrepresentations*]. However, there is always the chance of rebuilding the relationship severed by [*First and last name of* COMPANY *salesperson*]. Hopefully, [*Pronoun referring to salesperson's gender, i.e., "his" or "her"*] actions and unprofessional demeanor are not representative of your entire organization.

Sincerely yours,

[YOUR NAME]
[YOUR TITLE]

Missed Meeting Apology

TO: [*First and last name of person receiving memo*]

FROM: [YOUR NAME]
[YOUR TITLE]

DATE: [DATE]

SUBJECT: Apology

There are times in our lives when we make terrible mistakes. Afterwards, we realize that, if somehow given the chance to turn back the clock, our actions would have been different. Mistakes that affect only ourselves are far less important than those that influence others.

I am afraid you are the subject of my error in not attending the [*One or two words defining meeting's purpose*] meeting. No excuse could possibly convey my regret for such a display of unprofessionalism. I extend my sincerest apologies with the hope that this action will not reflect negatively on your opinion of my commitment to [YOUR COMPANY NAME].

If possible, I would like to obtain any information or notes resulting from the meeting. Please know that I have learned from this mistake and promise to maintain the professional standards of our company in the future.

cc: [COPIES TO]

Missed You at Seminar

[DATE]

[Mr./Mrs./Ms./Dr.] [CUSTOMER'S FULL NAME]
[CUSTOMER'S TITLE]
[COMPANY]
[ADDRESS]
[CITY], [STATE] [ZIP CODE]

Dear [Mr./Mrs./Ms./Dr.] [CUSTOMER'S LAST NAME]:

There was a friendly face missing in the crowd! Our event on [*Date event was held*] went well, and those who attended walked away with an armful of beneficial literature and a mind full of ideas. It is unfortunate that you were not able to attend and missed this opportunity to learn more about [*Describe most significant topic of seminar*].

At your convenience of course, it would be my pleasure to go over the highlights of the event with you. While I can't promise to be as effective as our expert presenters, I will do my very best. We have not scheduled another presentation like this for some time.

I will phone to set a time for a brief, informal presentation in the near future. Thank you in advance for sharing my excitement over [*Describe most significant topic of seminar*]. A recap of the cutting-edge advancements would surely be beneficial to both of us.

Sincerely yours,

[YOUR NAME]
[YOUR TITLE]

Mix up Apology

[DATE]

[Mr./Mrs./Ms./Dr.] [CUSTOMER'S FULL NAME]
[CUSTOMER'S TITLE]
[COMPANY]
[ADDRESS]
[CITY], [STATE] [ZIP CODE]

Dear [Mr./Mrs./Ms./Dr.] [CUSTOMER'S LAST NAME]:

Often, when things go wrong, far too much energy is wasted in finger-pointing. We are better served using those resources to solve the problem than worrying about who is to blame. [YOUR COMPANY NAME]'s standards do not permit game playing.

It really doesn't matter where the fault lies in [COMPANY]'s disappointment regarding [*Describe what happened*]. A disgruntled customer is always right. Steps have been taken to [*Describe actions* YOUR COMPANY NAME *is taking to fix mix up*].

Please accept my apologies and suggestion that we move forward and put this situation behind us. Thank you for your patience. [YOUR COMPANY NAME] doesn't waste time with games; we just work for 100 percent customer confidence.

Sincerely yours,

[YOUR NAME]
[YOUR TITLE]

Moderate Reminder

[DATE]

[Mr./Mrs./Ms./Dr.] [CUSTOMER'S FULL NAME]
[CUSTOMER'S TITLE]
[COMPANY]
[ADDRESS]
[CITY], [STATE] [ZIP CODE]

Dear [Mr./Mrs./Ms./Dr.] [CUSTOMER'S LAST NAME]:

Far too often, companies take credit extensions lightly, failing to consider that suppliers must carry the burden for late-paying customers. Both vendors and customers have obligations. Vendors provide high-quality goods and services; customers, in return, pay for those goods and services under the agreed upon terms.

[YOUR COMPANY NAME] has lived up to our side of the bargain; [COMPANY] has fallen behind. Because of [COMPANY]'s credit rating, we extended ourselves to the point of providing references when [COMPANY] applied for credit with other companies.

By sending $[*Dollar amount of payment needed from* COMPANY] immediately, you will make your account current and protect your credit rating. If this is not possible or extenuating circumstances prevent [COMPANY] from complying with our request for payment, please call me today. Good credit ratings take years to establish and only months to destroy. Thank you for your prompt attention. Professionals like us know that bad credit is very difficult to conceal. Don't let another day go by without addressing this issue.

Sincerely yours,

[YOUR NAME]
[YOUR TITLE]

Money-back Guarantee

[DATE]

[Mr./Mrs./Ms./Dr.] [CUSTOMER'S FULL NAME]
[CUSTOMER'S TITLE]
[COMPANY]
[ADDRESS]
[CITY], [STATE] [ZIP CODE]

Dear [Mr./Mrs./Ms./Dr.] [CUSTOMER'S LAST NAME]:

Most of us learn early that life offers few guarantees. No matter how much good faith and judgment we use in our decision making, we learn that change is inescapable. As a business, we recognize this and attempt to make life more manageable by offering a pledge of 100 percent customer satisfaction.

We honor our customer commitment with a money-back guarantee and stand behind this promise concerning your return of [*Name of product returned*]. Many praise this product, but we recognize that individual needs differ. Therefore, a complete refund has been processed for [COMPANY] and is [*Describe where the refund is or has been posted*].

We trust this action proves to [COMPANY] that there is at least one thing guaranteed in life and one company that truly understands the meaning of customer satisfaction. Hopefully, your faith has been restored, and our faithful adherence to our commitment will allow you to purchase from us again in the future.

Sincerely yours,

[YOUR NAME]
[YOUR TITLE]

Money-back Guarantee Return

[DATE]

[Mr./Mrs./Ms./Dr.] [FIRST AND LAST NAME]
[TITLE]
[COMPANY]
[ADDRESS]
[CITY], [STATE] [ZIP CODE]

Dear [Mr./Mrs./Ms./Dr.] [LAST NAME]:

Today, what you buy is not as important as whom you buy from. Customer satisfaction and operational goals are intertwined in companies of high ethical standing. I write in the hope that [COMPANY] recognizes the value of a customer as [YOUR COMPANY NAME] returns [*Name of product purchased*].

Based upon [COMPANY]'s claims of 100 percent satisfaction through a money-back guarantee, we willingly purchased [*Name of product purchased*] for $[*Dollar amount paid for product purchased*] on [*Date product was purchased*]. Simply stated, it does not meet our performance or quality expectations. The [*Name of product purchased*] is enclosed with this letter.

[YOUR COMPANY NAME] has already spent much time and effort acquiring [*Name of product purchased*]. It is my hope that no more of either will be required to receive our rightful 100 percent refund of the purchase price. Thank you for your prompt attention. We find reassurance in the fulfillment of supplier claims.

Sincerely yours,

[YOUR NAME]
[YOUR TITLE]

Monthly Sales Results Request

TO: [*First and last name of person receiving memo*]

FROM: [YOUR NAME]
[YOUR TITLE]

DATE: [DATE]

SUBJECT: Monthly Sales Request

Maintaining communication with the sales force is sometimes difficult. By all means, we want you to be with customers in the field or on the telephone helping customers gain additional insight about [YOUR COMPANY NAME]'s growing placement in the [*Describe the industry focus of* YOUR COMPANY NAME] industry.

Unless you take a moment out today for paperwork and tell us how you're doing with our customers, we'll never know how we can help you. Please prepare your monthly sales figures for the month of [*Month of the year sales results cover*] and have them in my office by [*Date monthly sales results are due*].

Specifically, list in chart form by customer name the following: [*Describe what you want to know*]. I am most interested in [*Describe the information most important to you*].

If you anticipate a problem getting the report in on time, let me know immediately. I look forward to spreading your success stories throughout the company.

cc: [COPIES TO]

Name Change Announcement

[DATE]

[Mr./Mrs./Ms./Dr.] [CUSTOMER'S FULL NAME]
[CUSTOMER'S TITLE]
[COMPANY]
[ADDRESS]
[CITY], [STATE] [ZIP CODE]

Dear [Mr./Mrs./Ms./Dr.] [CUSTOMER'S LAST NAME]:

Philosophers have for centuries contemplated the question, "What is a name?" What a name is, however, is not as important as what stands behind it. Therefore, we doubt that a name change from [YOUR COMPANY NAME] to [*New name of* YOUR COMPANY NAME] will mean very much to valued customers like [COMPANY].

Our business relationship has given you an insider's appreciation of our customer-oriented attitude and outstanding ethics. The new name merely serves as a better reflection of our successful positioning in the [*Describe* YOUR NEW COMPANY NAME's *main business emphasis*] industry. We know [COMPANY] stands behind us. After all, it does not really matter what we call ourselves. The inside, not the outside, is what counts.

Sincerely yours,

[YOUR NAME]
[YOUR TITLE]

Need Additional Bid Information

[DATE]

[Mr./Mrs./Ms./Dr.] [CUSTOMER'S FULL NAME]
[CUSTOMER'S TITLE]
[COMPANY]
[ADDRESS]
[CITY], [STATE] [ZIP CODE]

Dear [Mr./Mrs./Ms./Dr.] [CUSTOMER'S LAST NAME]:

When all is said and done, there can be only one winner of [COMPANY]'s bid for [*Describe what the bid is for*], number [*Provide* COMPANY's *bid tracking number for what the bid is for*]. I am positive that the decision committee has already formulated their evaluation criteria, among which, I am sure, is accuracy. [YOUR COMPANY NAME]'s primary goal in answering [COMPANY]'s bid request is to provide the information completely and clearly, according to your specifications.

We want your business without doubt or hesitation. But before we can provide a bid, we require the following additional information: [*Describe* YOUR COMPANY NAMEs *questions*].

Please either call or forward your interpretation of the above areas as soon as possible. Only then, will we be confident that our answers match your questions. Thank you for your prompt assistance. The [YOUR COMPANY NAME]-[COMPANY] account team is eager to finish the winning proposal.

Sincerely yours,

[YOUR NAME]
[YOUR TITLE]

Need Additional Information to Adjust

[DATE]

[Mr./Mrs./Ms./Dr.] [CUSTOMER'S FULL NAME]
[CUSTOMER'S TITLE]
[COMPANY]
[ADDRESS]
[CITY], [STATE] [ZIP CODE]

Dear [Mr./Mrs./Ms./Dr.] [CUSTOMER'S LAST NAME]:

A decision founded on fact rather than hearsay is optimum. This does not imply, however, that we ignore another's perspective before making a final judgment. For our mutual benefit, [YOUR COMPANY NAME] follows rigorous decision-making standards that include customer input.

Upon reviewing [COMPANY]'s file and your correspondence requesting an adjustment on [*Describe the adjustment request*], I find that we need more information.

We are missing facts and documentation that are essential to our prompt resolution of your problem. Specifically, [*Describe the information needed from* COMPANY] would substantiate [COMPANY]'s adjustment request and might facilitate a decision in your favor. Thank you for working with us to reach a resolution. You can anticipate a response within [*Length of time needed by* YOUR COMPANY NAME *to make decision*] of my receipt of the information.

Sincerely yours,

[YOUR NAME]
[YOUR TITLE]

Need Additional Time to Answer

[DATE]

[Mr./Mrs./Ms./Dr.] [CUSTOMER'S FULL NAME]
[CUSTOMER'S TITLE]
[COMPANY]
[ADDRESS]
[CITY], [STATE] [ZIP CODE]

Dear [Mr./Mrs./Ms./Dr.] [CUSTOMER'S LAST NAME]:

Jumping to conclusions often lands one in the slough of regret. On rare occasions, a customer presents [YOUR COMPANY NAME] with a problem to which an immediate response is not possible. Your criticism regarding [*Describe* COMPANY's *complaint*] is my responsibility, and you should know that our company is not ignoring it.

However, I need additional time to assure a thorough evaluation. I am starting at the beginning to uncover the conditions that placed a valued customer in such a situation.

You can be confident that I will move quickly, because customer satisfaction is one of our greatest priorities. You demand and deserve nothing less than the best. Thank you for your patience. I look forward to an amicable resolution.

Sincerely yours,

[YOUR NAME]
[YOUR TITLE]

Need Signature

[DATE]

[Mr./Mrs./Ms./Dr.] [CUSTOMER'S FULL NAME]
[CUSTOMER'S TITLE]
[COMPANY]
[ADDRESS]
[CITY], [STATE] [ZIP CODE]

Dear [Mr./Mrs./Ms./Dr.] [CUSTOMER'S LAST NAME]:

Sometimes in the daily hustle and bustle of business, the big picture gets our undivided attention. Occasionally, even an intelligent, influential individual like you will overlook a minor detail or two. We received the contract for [COMPANY]'s [*Describe the contract's purpose*], but one very critical item is missing.

Before we can proceed, page [*Page number of contract* COMPANY *must sign*] requires your signature. I know this is simply an oversight, and we'll be on our way just as soon as I receive the signed contract.

[COMPANY] has a reputation for never letting people down. However, should you foresee a problem in returning the contract within the next five days, please notify me of your plans. I'll need to undo the preparations I have made and the work already in progress to meet [COMPANY]'s needs. Thank you for your prompt attention.

Sincerely yours,

[YOUR NAME]
[YOUR TITLE]

Negative PR Critique

[DATE]

[Mr./Mrs./Ms./Dr.] [FIRST AND LAST NAME]
[TITLE]
[COMPANY]
[ADDRESS]
[CITY], [STATE] [ZIP CODE]

Dear [Mr./Mrs./Ms./Dr.] [LAST NAME]:

Journalists have a legal and moral responsibility to report accurately. Casebooks are full of decisions dealing with the consequences of gee-whiz headlines and sensational stories. I am confident that [COMPANY] is aware of the potential ramifications of incompetent reporting.

A person in your position clearly understands routine article research guidelines. I question whether the author, [*First and last name of author*], of the article about [YOUR COMPANY NAME] that appeared in your [*Date of publication*] issue knows the definition of professional ethics.

Specifically, "[*Select what you consider the worst sentence from article*]," is poor journalism. The coverage could have been made accurate by including [*Describe and list by number things that should have been in article*].

If there were any questions, these should have been brought to our attention before the piece was submitted for editorial review or publication. [*First and last name of author*]'s inaccurate reporting has hurt [COMPANY]'s reputation more than [YOUR COMPANY NAME]'s. Our clients, many of whom are your readers, know how to distinguish fact from fiction.

Sincerely yours,

[YOUR NAME]
[YOUR TITLE]

Negative Response Adjustment

[DATE]

[Mr./Mrs./Ms./Dr.] [CUSTOMER'S FULL NAME]
[CUSTOMER'S TITLE]
[COMPANY]
[ADDRESS]
[CITY], [STATE] [ZIP CODE]

Dear [Mr./Mrs./Ms./Dr.] [CUSTOMER'S LAST NAME]:

A customer's concern is our concern. Thank you for informing [YOUR COMPANY NAME] of a possible discrepancy regarding [COMPANY]'s [*Describe the issue on which* COMPANY *requested an adjustment*]. We encourage customers to contact us when such situations arise.

However, an extensive review of [COMPANY]'s records indicates that no mistakes were made and the [*Describe the issue on which* COMPANY *requested an adjustment*] is correct as stated. If you have discovered additional information about the situation, by all means, call or write again; your input will help us serve you better. We are always here when you need us, and we thank you for your past and future business.

Sincerely,

[YOUR NAME]
[YOUR TITLE]

New Appraisal Request

TO: [*First and last name of person receiving memo*]

FROM: [YOUR NAME]
[YOUR TITLE]

DATE: [DATE]

SUBJECT: Performance Appraisal Request Review

Objective opinion is sometimes swayed by subjective thought. Our individual backgrounds and experiences have a tendency to influence our judgments and perceptions. Remaining impartial and unbiased in our dealings can be difficult at times.

Allow me to illustrate. Let's assume that I wanted you to meet one of my friends. In one instance, I told you how often this person has helped me over the years. In the other instance, I told you how often this person has asked for money. In either case, you would have formed an opinion of my friend before ever shaking hands with him or her. This subjective impression would later be confirmed or denied when the introduction took place and you formed an objective judgment.

I may be wrong, but I believe that my performance appraisal for [*Time the performance appraisal covered, i.e., "second quarter," "1995," etc.*], contains misconceptions founded on hearsay rather than fact. I cannot tell you how many nights I have lain awake wondering what I could have done better or more effectively to benefit [YOUR COMPANY NAME]. After much deliberation, I decided to find out by taking the first step and asking for a review of my performance appraisal.

I seek additional insight into the criteria and methodology used by [YOUR COMPANY NAME] in determining performance levels. It has always been my goal to exceed my employer's expectations, and I believe that I performed my duties competently during [*Time the performance appraisal covered, i.e., "second quarter," "1995," etc.*]. Please let me know as soon as possible when we can meet. I thank you in advance for your professionalism in this matter.

cc: [COPIES TO]

New Employee Hired

TO: All Staff

FROM: [YOUR NAME]
[YOUR TITLE]

DATE: [DATE]

SUBJECT: Welcome Our Newest Employee, [*First and last name of person hired*]

It's hard being the new kid on the block. While getting coffee or walking through the office, you may have noticed a fresh face. Go up and introduce yourself to our new employee, [*First and last name of person hired*], who is a [*Title of person hired*] working with us to [*Job function of person hired*].

[*First name of person hired*] is a valuable addition to [YOUR COMPANY NAME], bringing many skills and talents to better our operation. I am confident each of you will agree as opportunities arise to work together. Today, please take a moment from your busy schedule to welcome [*First name of person hired*] to our company.

cc: [COPIES TO]

New Hire Reference Request

[DATE]

[Mr./Mrs./Ms./Dr.] [FIRST AND LAST NAME]
[TITLE]
[COMPANY]
[ADDRESS]
[CITY], [STATE] [ZIP CODE]

Dear [Mr./Mrs./Ms./Dr.] [LAST NAME]:

First impressions are not always reliable. While trusting your conscience has merit, hiring decisions require certainty. We want not only the most experienced, knowledgeable, and team-oriented people, but people who will fit in with our corporate culture.

A former employee of [COMPANY], [*First and last name of employee*], recently applied for a [*Position employee is applying for*] position with [YOUR COMPANY NAME] and gave your name as a reference.

In accordance with the law, please provide [*Pronoun referring to employee's gender, i.e., "his" or "her"*] dates of employment and salary history. Thank you in advance for your assistance in our hiring process. As I'm sure you know, we need all the help we can get with the challenging process of hiring new employees.

Sincerely yours,

[YOUR NAME]
[YOUR TITLE]

New Insurance Action Needed

[DATE]

[Mr./Mrs./Ms./Dr.] [FIRST AND LAST NAME]
[TITLE]
[COMPANY]
[ADDRESS]
[CITY], [STATE] [ZIP CODE]

Reference Claim Number: [*Claim number assigned to incident by* COMPANY]

Dear [Mr./Mrs./Ms./Dr.] [LAST NAME]:

Insurance. You pay for it. You may never need it. But when you do need it, you are supposed to be glad you have it. Reflecting back on [*Date event happened to be covered by insurance*] when [*Event that happened covered by insurance*], I found comfort in believing that [COMPANY] would abide by its promises of investment protection and loss minimization.

I want to continue to maintain that insurance makes misfortune more bearable. However, our company's experience with [COMPANY] makes me wonder if that belief is realistic. Pardon such frankness, but the settlement claim for [*Event that happened covered by insurance*] covered under policy number [YOUR COMPANY NAME's *insurance policy number assigned by* COMPANY] is aggravating, not easing, the pain of our misfortune.

There are apparently errors or omissions in the list of the damages that have caused an inadequate claim settlement. Glancing at the settlement description, the obvious errors include: [*Describe and list by number errors*]. It is my hope that [COMPANY] will take a proactive position resulting in an increased reimbursement. Only then, will a chance exist that [YOUR COMPANY NAME] will consider its insurance premiums money well spent. Thank you in advance for helping to increase our customer satisfaction.

Sincerely yours,

[YOUR NAME]
[YOUR TITLE]

New Job

[DATE]

[Mr./Mrs./Ms./Dr.] [CUSTOMER'S FULL NAME]
[CUSTOMER'S TITLE]
[COMPANY]
[ADDRESS]
[CITY], [STATE] [ZIP CODE]

Dear [Mr./Mrs./Ms./Dr.] [CUSTOMER'S LAST NAME]:

Many fear change and choose comfort over challenge. After all, it is easier to plod along in the familiar than to explore the unknown. I extend my congratulations to you for moving forward in your new position as [*Title of the new job*].

You have both the knowledge and the skills to excel. While the title may be nothing new to [COMPANY], your professionalism makes this position a corporate asset. If there is any way I can support you in this transition, just say the word.

Again, congratulations on the new job. I would wish you good luck, but I know it isn't necessary. Your talents already have things well-covered.

Sincerely yours,

[YOUR NAME]
[YOUR TITLE]

New Manager Review Request

TO: [*First and last name of person receiving memo*]

FROM: [YOUR NAME]
[YOUR TITLE]

DATE: [DATE]

SUBJECT: Management Review Request

Mentor relationships—parent-child, teacher-student, coach-player, manager-employee—exist throughout our lives. In every such relationship, the mentor must be willing to teach, and the student to learn. Both parties must agree on the depth and direction of the relationship and the goals they want to realize. Clearly, I am the student to [*First and last name of your manager*] in a student-teacher relationship.

Today, I can look at myself in the mirror and honestly say that I have tried earnestly in actions and words to make my professional relationship with [*First and last name of your manager*] work. Frankly, I don't think [*Pronoun referring to first and last name of your manager's gender, i.e., "he" or "she"*] can say the same. Under [*First name of your manager*]'s continued direction, my professional career will not be what is in my, or [YOUR COMPANY NAME]'s, best interest.

I trust you will keep my thoughts on the matter completely confidential until we personally discuss the details and possible alternatives. My concern has always been, and continues to be, for the company and for our team's success. Please call and let me know when we can meet. Thank you in advance for your professional courtesy and understanding; every winning player needs a good coach.

cc: [COPIES TO]

New Position Review Request

TO: [Full name of person receiving memo]

FROM: [YOUR NAME]
[YOUR TITLE]

DATE: [DATE]

SUBJECT: Position and Title Review Request

I relish the sort of professional challenge that makes my heart pump faster, keeps my mind alert, and calls forth my inner strength. These are truly invitations to test ambition, knowledge and skills. Thus far in my career, challenge has propelled me through success after success.

Today, the challenge has been met in my position as [*Title of the position you now hold*], creating the need to further my career ambitions. While this is not to imply that there is nothing left for me to learn, or no skill remaining to be perfected, I believe a transition to [*Title of the position you want*] would be beneficial.

To list all my accomplishments thus far on one page of typed text would not do them justice. There are many that demonstrate my ability, experience, and drive.

If given the opportunity to be [YOUR COMPANY NAME]'s newest [*Title of the position you want*], I would be the company's best defense against failure. You have my pledge that [YOUR COMPANY NAME] will not be disappointed. Thank you in advance for your consideration. I look forward to hearing your decision and welcoming the opportunity to prove further my worth as an employee and member of the [YOUR COMPANY NAME] team.

cc: [COPIES TO]

New Procedure

TO: [*First and last name of person receiving memo*]

FROM: [YOUR NAME]
[YOUR TITLE]

DATE: [DATE]

SUBJECT: New Procedures for [*One or two words describing procedure that changed*]

The shortest distance between two points is a straight line. Management has received many suggestions intended to help us streamline [*One or two words describing procedure that changed*].

Incorporating employee recommendations is beneficial to [YOUR COMPANY NAME]. Therefore, we have made adjustments to eliminate unnecessary steps in [*One or two words describing procedure that changed*]. Effective today, the procedure is as follows: [*Describe step-by-step procedure for amending procedure that changed*].

Should you have any questions on the new procedure, please do not hesitate to contact [*First and last name of person responsible for implementing new procedure*] at [*Telephone number for person responsible for implementing new procedure*]. As always, we appreciate those who care enough about [YOUR COMPANY NAME] to make suggestions. It truly is beneficial for our entire team.

cc: [COPIES TO]

New Sale

TO: [*First and last name of person receiving memo*]

FROM: [YOUR NAME]
[YOUR TITLE]

DATE: [DATE]

SUBJECT: New Sale at [*Name of the customer*]

On the narrow decks of aircraft carriers, pilots routinely land their jet-powered planes with incredible precision. The only thing stopping the jet's 100 mile per hour approach are steel cables across the deck. These landings are considered to be among the most difficult in aviation.

The pilots use a combination of expertise, knowledge, and skill to defy gravity. One wrong move could end in destruction.

Similarly, your handling of the [*Name of the customer*] account took great diligence and skill. Maneuvering through the sales cycle with such excellence is quite an accomplishment. You are a "Top Gun" in our company, where the sky is truly the limit. Congratulations on your success.

cc: [COPIES TO]

New Sales Representative Anouncement

[DATE]

[Mr./Mrs./Ms./Dr.] [CUSTOMER'S FULL NAME]
[CUSTOMER'S TITLE]
[COMPANY]
[ADDRESS]
[CITY], [STATE] [ZIP CODE]

Dear [Mr./Mrs./Ms./Dr.] [CUSTOMER'S LAST NAME]:

Every year, the National Football League commands much attention as teams pick their superstars and starting line-ups for the new season. We haven't hired a football star, but we have come very close with our newest marketing team member, [*First and last name of new salesperson*].

[*First name of new salesperson*]'s extensive background and experience promotes excellence for our company, customers, and fans. [YOUR COMPANY NAME] has confidence in [*First name of new salesperson*]'s ability to serve you in the most competent and professional manner possible. Soon, [*Pronoun referring to new salesperson's gender, i.e., "he" or "she"*] will visit [COMPANY]'s offices, and I am sure you'll approve of [YOUR COMPANY NAME]'s newest first string choice. We searched long and hard for this all-star player.

Sincerely yours,

[YOUR NAME]
[YOUR TITLE]

New Salesperson Request

[DATE]

[Mr./Mrs./Ms./Dr.] [FIRST AND LAST NAME]
[TITLE]
[COMPANY]
[ADDRESS]
[CITY], [STATE] [ZIP CODE]

Dear [Mr./Mrs./Ms./Dr.] [LAST NAME]:

We like to surround ourselves with knowledgeable and reputable winners. Assisting the next generation is equally important too. It's unfortunate that not all students recognize mentors in their professional lives.

One's immediate manager is not the sole source of practical education; a customer can teach too. My patience has worn increasingly thin with [*First and last name of* COMPANY's *sales representative* YOUR COMPANY NAME *wants to replace*]. I have neither the desire nor the authority to assume a disciplinary role. Trust me when I say that it is to [COMPANY]'s advantage that a new sales representative is assigned to handle [YOUR COMPANY NAME]'s business.

Rehashing the past is not always a productive venture. I'll just tell you [*First and last name of* COMPANY's *sales representative* YOUR COMPANY NAME *wants to replace*] needs remedial training in professional business practices. This is [COMPANY]'s task, not mine. I look forward to helping another representative develop his or her career. Hopefully, he or she will understand that learning is a life-long process and customer satisfaction is the highest priority.

Sincerely yours,

[YOUR NAME]
[YOUR TITLE]

No Payment to Speaker Invitation

[DATE]

[Mr./Mrs./Ms./Dr.] [FIRST AND LAST NAME]
[TITLE]
[COMPANY]
[ADDRESS]
[CITY], [STATE] [ZIP CODE]

Dear [Mr./Mrs./Ms./Dr.] [LAST NAME]:

A person of your expertise and stature has probably heard this story once or twice before. It starts out with an invitation to speak at a conference. Then you hear how you can help the audience, expand your contact base, increase your visibility, and improve your skills.

I am not disputing the validity of any of the above claims. You already know, probably better than I, that speaking engagements do all these things and more. You also know how often payment arrangements are made only to be canceled at the last minute when conference organizers discover that there is no money in the budget for your compensation.

[YOUR COMPANY NAME] is faced with wanting your skills at our [*Name of conference*] on [*Date of conference*] at [*Location of conference*] but not having any funds available. I see no need to give you a complete sales pitch that may insult your obvious intelligence. However, I do ask you to consider the advantages of spreading your message to so many people in such a setting. Please telephone me soon with a decision so that I can make alternate plans if you are unable to accommodate us. It would be an honor to have you participate in our event.

Sincerely yours,

[YOUR NAME]
[YOUR TITLE]

No Record of Return

[DATE]

[Mr./Mrs./Ms./Dr.] [CUSTOMER'S FULL NAME]
[CUSTOMER'S TITLE]
[COMPANY]
[ADDRESS]
[CITY], [STATE] [ZIP CODE]

Dear [Mr./Mrs./Ms./Dr.] [CUSTOMER'S LAST NAME]:

Not too long ago, businesses tracked activities quite reliably with pen and paper. Computer automation has made all that paperwork seem antiquated. Interestingly, most packages sent throughout the world now carry electronic bar codes that include the package's destination and the date it was shipped.

[YOUR COMPANY NAME] has spent a great deal of time and effort checking and double-checking our computer system and our receiving department's records for any sign of [COMPANY]'s return of [*Name of product supposedly returned*]. So far, nothing has turned up, leading us to believe that the goods have not been received. We have no alternative but to direct the search back to you in hopes that the missing goods may turn up elsewhere.

Contrary to popular belief, the fastest way to get between two points is not always a straight line. The key is finding where the line bent to the left or right. Thank you in advance for helping us come to a quick resolution of this matter.

Sincerely yours,

[YOUR NAME]
[YOUR TITLE]

No Replacement Offered

[DATE]

[Mr./Mrs./Ms./Dr.] [CUSTOMER'S FULL NAME]
[CUSTOMER'S TITLE]
[COMPANY]
[ADDRESS]
[CITY], [STATE] [ZIP CODE]

Dear [Mr./Mrs./Ms./Dr.] [CUSTOMER'S LAST NAME]:

Accept no substitutes. These words reverberate through my mind as I recall the last [YOUR COMPANY NAME] product meeting. Management did not have to think long about what to do with orders for [*Describe the unavailable product*].

Selling an inferior product definitely was out of the question. Continuing to be straightforward with our customers was the only answer. Therefore, I regret to report that [COMPANY]'s order for [*Describe the unavailable product*], placed on [*Date* COMPANY *placed order for the unavailable product*], cannot be filled at this time.

We all wish [YOUR COMPANY NAME] could change manufacturing's decision. Until there is a product comparable in quality and price, all we can do is be honest and do everything we can to uphold our reputation. I appreciate these characteristics in my business dealings. [YOUR COMPANY NAME] hopes you do too. Thank you for understanding. When we do find another [*Describe the unavailable product*], you'll be the first to receive a telephone call.

Sincerely yours,

[YOUR NAME]
[YOUR TITLE]

No Response to Inquiry

[DATE]

[Mr./Mrs./Ms./Dr.] [FIRST AND LAST NAME]
[TITLE]
[COMPANY]
[ADDRESS]
[CITY], [STATE] [ZIP CODE]

Dear [Mr./Mrs./Ms./Dr.] [LAST NAME]:

When a person inadvertently ingests a poisonous substance, we are taught to act quickly. The poison must be removed before damage is done. Accordingly, responses to our inquiries concerning unconventional business practices demand immediate attention.

I have contacted [COMPANY] on several occasions regarding [*Describe the outstanding issue*]. As a professional, I know this is not an insurmountable dilemma once the proper resources are dedicated. The key is making our concern a [COMPANY] priority by giving it attention.

[YOUR COMPANY NAME]'s stance has not changed. We still insist that [*Subject of the outstanding issue*] be [*Describe and list by number actions* COMPANY *must take to resolve the outstanding issue*] as soon as possible. Let's not waste any more valuable time; your unprofessionalism is destroying any possibility of future business with [YOUR COMPANY NAME]. I hope to hear from [COMPANY] within the next week with confirmation that the issue has been resolved to our mutual satisfaction. You know what it feels like when you're ignored.

Sincerely yours,

[YOUR NAME]
[YOUR TITLE]

Nondisclosure Agreement

Representatives of [YOUR COMPANY NAME], hereinafter referred to as "[YOUR COMPANY NAME]," and representatives of [COMPANY], hereinafter referred to as "Organization,"are discussing and meeting for the purpose of [YOUR COMPANY NAME] sharing confidential and/or proprietary information relating to [*Describe and list by number the subject requiring nondisclosure*]. Any and all discussions, presentations, and meetings may include information regarding company and/or product specifications, availability, pricing, marketing, and business data, all of which are considered proprietary information of [YOUR COMPANY NAME]. Organization agrees that all information it receives from [YOUR COMPANY NAME] at any time concerning [*Describe and list by number the subject requiring nondisclosure*] or related plans will be treated in a confidential manner, will not be used except as authorized, and will not be disclosed to any third party. Organization will be released from the above obligations when the information and/or products are announced by [YOUR COMPANY NAME]. Confidential disclosure of information relating to unreleased company and/or product specifications does not imply an undertaking that any future activities will necessarily conform to specifications, prices, or availability dates disclosed under this Agreement.

[YOUR COMPANY NAME]

______________________________	______________________________
Authorized Representative's Printed Name	Title
______________________________	______________________________
Signature	Date

Organization

______________________________	______________________________
Authorized Representative's Printed Name	Title
______________________________	______________________________
Signature	Date

Nondisclosure Policy

TO: [*First and last name of person receiving memo*]

FROM: [YOUR NAME]
[YOUR TITLE]

DATE: [DATE]

SUBJECT: Nondisclosure

Information holds great power. Because security is its weapon, we need to respect the manner in which proprietary [YOUR COMPANY NAME] information is discussed and handled. Your efforts on [*Describe the activity the name of person receiving memo is working on with confidential or proprietary information*] increase the entire company's vulnerability to inappropriate disclosure.

While I know you would never let such a thing happen, we cannot afford even the appearance of impropriety. Please be aware that any and all discussions, presentations, and meetings that may include confidential or proprietary [YOUR COMPANY NAME] information must be approved beforehand by [*Person responsible for approval of information*].

We trust that all information concerning [*Describe the activity the name of person receiving memo is working on with confidential or proprietary information*] and related plans will be treated in a confidential manner and used only as authorized. Your compliance is mandatory. We wouldn't want this information to get into the wrong hands.

cc: [COPIES TO]

Non-receipt of Order

[DATE]

[Mr./Mrs./Ms./Dr.] [FIRST AND LAST NAME]
[TITLE]
[COMPANY]
[ADDRESS]
[CITY], [STATE] [ZIP CODE]

Dear [Mr./Mrs./Ms./Dr.] [LAST NAME]:

Our lives are becoming increasingly globally oriented. It's routine to expect a package originating in Los Angeles to arrive at its London destination in no more than 48 hours. We are no longer amazed at such a display of coordination and advanced technology.

I am concerned that [YOUR COMPANY NAME]'s order placed on [*Date order was placed*] has not been received. Specifically, we requested shipment of [*Describe and list by number order's contents*]. [COMPANY] promises timely delivery of all customer orders, and this situation is not consistent with your customer satisfaction commitments.

Believing that [COMPANY] may not be aware of this situation, I call it to your attention. Please advise me on the status of our order immediately. Thank you for your assistance and prompt reply. I would like to use the [*Product*] soon.

Sincerely yours,

[YOUR NAME]
[YOUR TITLE]

Not Your Company's Fault

[DATE]

[Mr./Mrs./Ms./Dr.] [CUSTOMER'S FULL NAME]
[CUSTOMER'S TITLE]
[COMPANY]
[ADDRESS]
[CITY], [STATE] [ZIP CODE]

Dear [Mr./Mrs./Ms./Dr.] [CUSTOMER'S LAST NAME]:

The simplest transaction becomes complex when a misunderstanding clouds the issue. Words are so easily taken out of context. After thoroughly reviewing your criticism about [*Describe* COMPANY's *complaint*], I gathered my findings and presented them at our internal quality assurance meeting.

I realize the results are not what you want to hear. However, we reaffirm [YOUR COMPANY NAME]'s commitment to excellence in customer service. In addition, because no wrongful acts were done, I cannot offer restitution in the matter.

This decision was based primarily on [*Describe the major reason* COMPANY's *complaint is not* YOUR COMPANY NAME's *fault*]. Although we cannot accept responsibility, we want you to understand that all transactions are important to us. Thank you for taking [YOUR COMPANY NAME]'s word as honorable. We value good customers like [COMPANY] and hope this response does not impair our business affiliation.

Sincerely yours,

[YOUR NAME]
[YOUR TITLE]

Office Equipment Inquiry

[DATE]

[Mr./Mrs./Ms./Dr.] [FIRST AND LAST NAME]
[TITLE]
[COMPANY]
[ADDRESS]
[CITY], [STATE] [ZIP CODE]

Dear [Mr./Mrs./Ms./Dr.] [LAST NAME]:

Picture running a company in today's fast-moving environment with early 20th century tools. There were no copy machines, no overnight package deliveries, no ways to access information instantaneously, and telephone service was shaky at best. These devices and services, along with many others, have developed over time into business advantages and necessities.

To remain competitive, [YOUR COMPANY NAME] has determined a probable need to lease or purchase a [*Describe and list by number office equipment* YOUR COMPANY NAME *needs*]. Therefore, I am requesting information on cost-effective ways to meet our current and future business requirements.

Please have a [COMPANY] sales representative contact me and arrange a time to evaluate our present requirements. The best time to call is around [*Time of day you would like to receive* COMPANY's *telephone call*]. I look forward to hearing from [COMPANY] in the near future.

One can only surmise what office equipment will be like 100 years from now. What will a citizen of the late 21st century think of today's high-tech tools? Undoubtedly, great change is an accurate prediction.

Sincerely yours,

[YOUR NAME]
[YOUR TITLE]

Open House

[DATE]

[Mr./Mrs./Ms./Dr.] [CUSTOMER'S FULL NAME]
[CUSTOMER'S TITLE]
[COMPANY]
[ADDRESS]
[CITY], [STATE] [ZIP CODE]

Dear [Mr./Mrs./Ms./Dr.] [CUSTOMER'S LAST NAME]:

We blink our eyes about 84,000,000 times every year. Because it happens so fast, we see just about everything that falls within our field of vision. However, there are many more facets to [YOUR COMPANY NAME] than meet the eye.

From the highest executive ranks to the invaluable operational staff, we are separately and collectively proud of our efficient corporation. On [*Date of open house*] beginning at [*Time open house begins*], we are opening the doors to our most treasured customers.

I hope you will accept our invitation and share our vision. Please R.S.V.P. by [*Describe how and whom to contact to R.S.V.P.*] no later than [*Date person receiving letter should R.S.V.P. by*]. We want you to see us up close and personal.

Sincerely yours,

[YOUR NAME]
[YOUR TITLE]

Opportunity Not Acknowledged

[DATE]

[Mr./Mrs./Ms./Dr.] [FIRST AND LAST NAME]
[TITLE]
[COMPANY]
[ADDRESS]
[CITY], [STATE] [ZIP CODE]

Dear [Mr./Mrs./Ms./Dr.] [LAST NAME]:

Abner Doubleday is given credit for inventing baseball, but Egyptians as far back as 3022 B.C. played the game. Those first games using a melon and shepherd's staff laid the foundation for today's big leagues. The point is that before anything can happen, someone must throw the first pitch.

Opportunities become successes when action is taken. Recently, I sent you a letter expressing interest in [YOUR COMPANY NAME]'s potential collaboration with [COMPANY]. I saw the beginning of a mutually beneficial relationship to [*Describe business opportunity presented in letter*]. To date, I have not had a reply and am curious as to whether my correspondence dated [*Date of letter opportunity was first presented to* COMPANY] was received.

Together, we could create the newest American legend, much like Mom, apple pie, and baseball. We have stepped up to the plate and are ready to play ball. Thank you in advance for your professional courtesy. I am waiting for [COMPANY] to enter the field by telephoning and expressing interest in discussing the matter.

Sincerely yours,

[YOUR NAME]
[YOUR TITLE]

Opportunity Request

[DATE]

[Mr./Mrs./Ms./Dr.] [CUSTOMER'S FULL NAME]
[CUSTOMER'S TITLE]
[COMPANY]
[ADDRESS]
[CITY], [STATE] [ZIP CODE]

Dear [Mr./Mrs./Ms./Dr.] [CUSTOMER'S LAST NAME]:

It makes sound business sense to evaluate all available sources before selecting a vendor. [YOUR COMPANY NAME] recently became aware that [COMPANY] has released a bid for [*Describe what the bid is for*], number [*Provide* COMPANY's *bid tracking number for what the bid is for*], requesting that potential vendors provide product and pricing information. We hope to be included in this, and all future, bid opportunities.

Please send complete bid specifications to my attention at: [YOUR COMPANY NAME's *address*]. I have a special request because of your expertise in operational needs. For some time, [YOUR COMPANY NAME] has built a solid foundation providing superior service and [*Describe* YOUR COMPANY NAME's *main business emphasis*] products for companies just like yours.

Should there be any other outstanding bids you believe might complement our business, I would appreciate the opportunity to give these my professional attention as well. Thank you for your assistance. [YOUR COMPANY NAME] is everything you always wanted in a vendor, and we have the track record to prove it.

Sincerely yours,

[YOUR NAME]
[YOUR TITLE]

Order Confirmation

[DATE]

[Mr./Mrs./Ms./Dr.] [CUSTOMER'S FULL NAME]
[CUSTOMER'S TITLE]
[COMPANY]
[ADDRESS]
[CITY], [STATE] [ZIP CODE]

Dear [Mr./Mrs./Ms./Dr.] [CUSTOMER'S LAST NAME]:

Fewer than 20 percent of the diamonds mined annually reach gem status. Cut and polished by expert hands, diamonds take on worth based on their color, clarity, cut, and weight. I like to think that [YOUR COMPANY NAME] is one of the most valuable business resources a company can have.

Your order for [*Describe what the order was for*] confirmed that we are handling your account with care and competence. If there is anything I can do, please remember that you are my customer. [*First name of person receiving letter*], thank you for trusting me to keep your best interest in mind. When you are successful, I am too. After all, the best diamonds reflect the most light.

Sincerely yours,

[YOUR NAME]
[YOUR TITLE]

Outline of Meeting

TO: [*First and last name of person receiving memo*]

FROM: [YOUR NAME]
[YOUR TITLE]

DATE: [DATE]

SUBJECT: [*One or two words defining meeting*] Meeting Outline

When more than one topic is to be discussed in a relatively brief time, preparation can contribute immeasurably to the overall efficiency of the meeting. This is especially true in intricate matters like [*One or two words defining meeting*]. Therefore, I am providing a topical outline for our upcoming meeting, so you can gather supporting materials that will allow us to deal with the subject thoroughly and quickly.

To date, our respective expertise and input have been very beneficial in reaching a consensus on some outstanding issues. Areas that require further deliberation and investigation include the following: [*Describe up to five separate meeting points to cover*].

Please bring your documentation and ideas concerning the above to the meeting. As a reminder, we are meeting promptly at [*Time the meeting begins*] in [*Place within office where meeting will be held*]. If you have any questions or items to add to the outline, do not hesitate to contact me. Your suggestions for increasing [YOUR COMPANY NAME]'s productivity are always welcome.

cc: [COPIES TO]

Over Account Limit

[DATE]

[Mr./Mrs./Ms./Dr.] [CUSTOMER'S FULL NAME]
[CUSTOMER'S TITLE]
[COMPANY]
[ADDRESS]
[CITY], [STATE] [ZIP CODE]

Dear [Mr./Mrs./Ms./Dr.] [CUSTOMER'S LAST NAME]:

Have you ever gone to the grocery store for just a handful of things and returned with more than one full grocery bag? If you're like most people, you frequently spend more than you plan to. Based on [COMPANY]'s recent order activity, it may be time to raise your credit with [YOUR COMPANY NAME].

[COMPANY]'s order placed on [*Date order was placed*], for [*Describe what the order was for*], exceeded the $[*Dollar amount of* COMPANY's *maximum allowable credit*] charge authorization level on your account by $[*Dollar amount* COMPANY *is over maximum allowable credit*]. The easiest and quickest way to work around this problem is to remit $[*Dollar amount* COMPANY *must pay to resume credit privileges*] immediately.

In no time at all, the order will be on its way. I would, however, like to prevent any future inconvenience. I recommend updating your credit profile so our accounting department can evaluate the possibility of increasing your credit line. The application can be processed when [COMPANY]'s outstanding balance is $[*Dollar amount of* COMPANY's *outstanding balance that* YOUR COMPANY NAME *wants before considering an increase in allowable credit*]. Please let me know as soon as possible what you would like us to do. We want smooth sailing now and in the future.

Sincerely yours,

[YOUR NAME]
[YOUR TITLE]

Overtime Policy

TO: All Staff

FROM: [YOUR NAME]
[YOUR TITLE]

DATE: [DATE]

SUBJECT: Overtime

Enthusiasm for one's work is an admirable characteristic. It is often the factor that separates a job from a job done well. [YOUR COMPANY NAME] is proud that so many employees devote themselves to the pursuit of excellence. The responsibilities associated with each job in the company have been assigned with the standard 40-hour workweek in mind.

Realizing that there can be extenuating circumstances that call for additional effort, [YOUR COMPANY NAME] compensates our employees accordingly. Working beyond regularly scheduled hours is done on a strictly volunteer basis. The overtime rate is [*How overtime is calculated, i.e., "one," or "one and a half," "two," etc.*] times the normal hourly rate for hours worked after the regular workday ends.

However, all overtime is subject to prior authorization. Failure to work overtime scheduled or not obtaining proper approvals may result in disciplinary action, up to and including dismissal.

In fairness to all employees, these overtime policies must be followed. Please do not let the guidelines impair your enthusiasm. We appreciate your willingness to sacrifice personal time in pursuit of corporate goals.

cc: [COPIES TO]

Partnership with Customer Emphasis

[DATE]

[Mr./Mrs./Ms./Dr.] [CUSTOMER'S FULL NAME]
[CUSTOMER'S TITLE]
[COMPANY]
[ADDRESS]
[CITY], [STATE] [ZIP CODE]

Dear [Mr./Mrs./Ms./Dr.] [CUSTOMER'S LAST NAME]:

Of all the wonders of the deep, I am especially fond of the relationship between the clown fish and the sea anemone. The bright orange clown fish lives inside the waving, stinging tentacles of the sea anemone.

The clown fish and the sea anemone have no chance for survival separately. Therefore, they have formed a partnership that allows them to live side by side. The bright orange color attracts prey into the tentacles, and the two organisms share the meal.

We have the makings of a similarly beneficial partnership. In keeping with our customer satisfaction goals, [YOUR COMPANY NAME] has competitively priced [*Describe* YOUR COMPANY NAME's *main business emphasis and what you are trying to market to* COMPANY]. [COMPANY] needs excellent service and product quality to remain competitive.

Today, it is a mystery to me why [COMPANY] would select any company but [YOUR COMPANY NAME]. Thank you in advance for letting me know what I can do to reinforce our future. If given the chance, we could survive as a team against all competitive odds.

Sincerely yours,

[YOUR NAME]
[YOUR TITLE]

Past Customer

[DATE]

[Mr./Mrs./Ms./Dr.] [CUSTOMER'S FULL NAME]
[CUSTOMER'S TITLE]
[COMPANY]
[ADDRESS]
[CITY], [STATE] [ZIP CODE]

Dear [Mr./Mrs./Ms./Dr.] [CUSTOMER'S LAST NAME]:

This morning's office commute was very typical of most days. The coffee, traffic, and radio disk jockey reminded me that another day had begun. Between traffic lights, I thought of our business relationship, which ended for no apparent reason.

In my mind, I replayed our conversations and meetings looking for clues. Was it price? Was it service? Maybe they just found a better deal elsewhere.

Whatever the reason, I write to let you know that I want to win back your confidence in our company. Let's talk about what happened and the things we can do to reestablish the relationship. I look forward to receiving your call, and I hope to be driving to your office some morning soon.

Sincerely yours,

[YOUR NAME]
[YOUR TITLE]

Past Support

[DATE]

[Mr./Mrs./Ms./Dr.] [CUSTOMER'S FULL NAME]
[CUSTOMER'S TITLE]
[COMPANY]
[ADDRESS]
[CITY], [STATE] [ZIP CODE]

Dear [Mr./Mrs./Ms./Dr.] [CUSTOMER'S LAST NAME]:

Have you ever noticed the camaraderie among NBA players on the basketball court? In the spirit of competition, players applaud their teammates; it doesn't matter whether they are watching a winning basket or a missed free throw. The effort expended is worthy of support and recognition.

I believe this example parallels our teamwork over the past [*Length of time you have known person receiving letter*]. Your endorsement of my efforts, during both good and bad times, is appreciated and extends beyond mere reinforcement. More important, it increases my desire for us to be the winning team.

Medals and plaques are unimportant to me. A higher accolade is simply knowing I am a valued player on the court of your business life. Thank you for supporting my efforts and allowing us to become friends and teammates.

Sincerely yours,

[YOUR NAME]
[YOUR TITLE]

Payment Enclosed

[DATE]

[Mr./Mrs./Ms./Dr.] [FIRST AND LAST NAME]
[TITLE]
[COMPANY]
[ADDRESS]
[CITY], [STATE] [ZIP CODE]

Dear [Mr./Mrs./Ms./Dr.] [LAST NAME]:

Accounts receivable controls and maintenance are necessary for efficient business operations. [YOUR COMPANY NAME] appreciates prompt payment from our customers and assumes that [COMPANY] does too.

In fulfilling our commitment, enclosed is $[*Dollar amount of payment made with the enclosed check*], check number [*Number on* YOUR COMPANY NAME *check*], for invoice number [*Invoice number issued by* COMPANY *for payment*]. Our records show that this payment brings our balance to $[*Balance on* YOUR COMPANY NAME *account with* COMPANY]. Should our calculations be in error, please contact me immediately. Thank you for your assistance in posting this payment to our account.

Sincerely yours,

[YOUR NAME]
[YOUR TITLE]

Payment for Speaker Invitation

[DATE]

[Mr./Mrs./Ms./Dr.] [FIRST AND LAST NAME]
[TITLE]
[COMPANY]
[ADDRESS]
[CITY], [STATE] [ZIP CODE]

Dear [Mr./Mrs./Ms./Dr.] [LAST NAME]:

The voices of influential people have commanded attention throughout history. From the first entertainers to present-day politicians, a few special people have the unique ability to spark enthusiasm in their audiences. Everything I have heard about your talents confirms that you share this ability with some of our great leaders.

Fortunately, our paths have crossed. I am pleased to extend a formal invitation to you to use your professional talents at [YOUR COMPANY NAME]'s [*Name of conference*] on [*Date of conference*]. As agreed, we will pay you $[*Amount speaker will be paid*].

To help you tailor your speech, responses received thus far suggest that the attendee profile is as follows: [*Describe and list by number average attendee's professional characteristics*]. While your knowledge of [*Topic of speech*] is a definite advantage, extra emphasis on [*Describe and list by number additional ideas to incorporate in topic of speech*] would be also well-received. Thank you for calling with confirmation and for giving us the honor of placing your name on our agenda.

Sincerely yours,

[YOUR NAME]
[YOUR TITLE]

Payment Refusal

[DATE]

[Mr./Mrs./Ms./Dr.] [FIRST AND LAST NAME]
[TITLE]
[COMPANY]
[ADDRESS]
[CITY], [STATE] [ZIP CODE]

Dear [Mr./Mrs./Ms./Dr.] [LAST NAME]:

Customer dissatisfaction is like a microscope that magnifies a company's inner workings. We learn the most about a company when it is presented with a problem. The manner in which problems are handled allows customers to decide whether a company is worthy of their business.

On [*Date incident occurred*], [YOUR COMPANY NAME] agreed with [COMPANY] to *[Describe the reason* YOUR COMPANY NAME *called upon* COMPANY]. Instead, we ended up with [*Describe the result of the reason* YOUR COMPANY NAME *called upon* COMPANY]. [COMPANY] was quick to ask for payment without any regard for our satisfaction or lack thereof. I will not authorize payment until [COMPANY] does the following: [*Describe and list by number actions* YOUR COMPANY NAME *wants* COMPANY *to take*].

There are no alternatives; there are no compromises. This is not a negotiation. [YOUR COMPANY NAME]'s success has been built on customer satisfaction levels that promote repeat business. Our recent experience with your company has left us disgusted and puzzled. I expect you to recognize the urgency of the matter and reply within the next five business days. I don't really like what I have seen so far.

Sincerely yours,

[YOUR NAME]
[YOUR TITLE]

Payment Stopped on Check

[DATE]

[Mr./Mrs./Ms./Dr.] [FIRST AND LAST NAME]
[TITLE]
[COMPANY]
[ADDRESS]
[CITY], [STATE] [ZIP CODE]

Dear [Mr./Mrs./Ms./Dr.] [LAST NAME]:

Reaction normally requires more time and money than an initial proactive stance. However, receipt of new information sometimes forces drastic measures to correct unforeseen problems. At [YOUR COMPANY NAME]'s effort and expense, we have taken actions regarding our recent payment to [COMPANY].

On [*Date product or service was purchased*], we ordered [*Describe the product or service purchased from* COMPANY] from [COMPANY] for $[*Dollar amount of the product or service purchased from* COMPANY]. Payment was processed, but after mailing the check, I received some disheartening news. Because [*Describe the product or service purchased from* COMPANY] is [*Describe and list by number problems with the product or service purchased*], payment has been stopped on check number [*Number of* YOUR COMPANY NAME *check*].

Based on the above information, I am positive that [COMPANY] understands the reactionary position assumed by [YOUR COMPANY NAME]. Thank you in advance for your professional reply. Our company's intention is to resolve this issue. I wait for your suggestions on renewing our confidence as a [COMPANY] customer.

Sincerely yours,

[YOUR NAME]
[YOUR TITLE]

Payment Upon Order Completion

[DATE]

[Mr./Mrs./Ms./Dr.] [FIRST AND LAST NAME]
[TITLE]
[COMPANY]
[ADDRESS]
[CITY], [STATE] [ZIP CODE]

Dear [Mr./Mrs./Ms./Dr.] [LAST NAME]:

Except for Robert's Rules of Order governing corporate boardroom etiquette, few books exist on business manners. Acceptable professional conduct is primarily a combination of common sense and past experience. Unfortunately, [COMPANY]'s request for payment on invoice number [*Invoice number from* COMPANY] falls outside conventional [YOUR COMPANY NAME] standards.

We do not expect our customers to remit payment on incomplete orders. Nor do we release funds until our vendors fulfill their obligations. When [YOUR COMPANY NAME]'s order for [*Describe the order referenced by invoice number from* COMPANY] is complete and passes quality assurance standards, payment will be processed promptly. As of this date, [*Describe and list by number what is missing from the order referenced by the above mentioned invoice number*] has not arrived.

Maintaining the highest customer satisfaction level is important to [YOUR COMPANY NAME]. The many books that exist on this subject have the common theme of putting customer priorities first. Thank you for your professional courtesy in the matter. Our goal now is to receive a complete order. Then, we can help you achieve your goal of obtaining payment.

Sincerely yours,

[YOUR NAME]
[YOUR TITLE]

Permission to Use as a Referral

[DATE]

[Mr./Mrs./Ms./Dr.] [CUSTOMER'S FULL NAME]
[CUSTOMER'S TITLE]
[COMPANY]
[ADDRESS]
[CITY], [STATE] [ZIP CODE]

Dear [Mr./Mrs./Ms./Dr.] [CUSTOMER'S LAST NAME]:

People are justifiably tired of marketing claims and want real-life examples. Who is better able to tell a vendor's story than a current customer? Thank you for your willingness to share [COMPANY]'s favorable experiences.

Your credible professional endorsement regarding our [*Describe* YOUR COMPANY NAME's *main business emphasis and what you are trying to market to* COMPANY *for an endorsement*] was a definite push in the right direction. While it's too soon to predict the outcome, there was no confusion regarding which company [*Name of company referred to* COMPANY *for an endorsement*] should buy from. [*First name of person receiving letter*], thank you for your assistance. I can't tell you how much I appreciate your support of my goals.

Sincerely yours,

[YOUR NAME]
[YOUR TITLE]

Permission to Use Copyrighted Material

[DATE]

[Mr./Mrs./Ms./Dr.] [FIRST AND LAST NAME]
[TITLE]
[COMPANY]
[ADDRESS]
[CITY], [STATE] [ZIP CODE]

Dear [Mr./Mrs./Ms./Dr.] [LAST NAME]:

We respect the copyright laws governing original works and request your permission to use the following in [YOUR COMPANY NAME]'s [*Describe reason for obtaining copyright permission*].

Author, Copyright Date, & Title: [*List the author, copyright date, title, and publication*]

Pages: [*Provide the page numbers where the author, copyright date, title, and publication can be found*]

Please acknowledge that this permission is granted by completing the bottom portion of this letter and returning one copy to my attention. Your signature confirms that you control the rights to this work and that it does not infringe on any other copyrights. Should you grant permission, we will include a permission line: "Reprinted by courtesy of [COMPANY]."

If for some reason you do not control this copyright, I would appreciate knowing whom I should contact. Thank you for your professional assistance. I am sure the author spent much time on the work and deserves credit for the effort.

Sincerely yours,

[YOUR NAME]
[YOUR TITLE]

Accepted by:

Signature________________________

Date____________________________

Copyright credit and/or notice as printed with material used:

Personal Appearance

TO: [*First and last name of person receiving memo*]

FROM: [YOUR NAME]
[YOUR TITLE]

DATE: [DATE]

SUBJECT: Personal Appearance

Your personal appearance is a direct reflection of your inner appearance. Like aspirations and goals, dress, grooming, and personal cleanliness contribute to one's professional image. [YOUR COMPANY NAME] has standards of acceptable business attire that have been developed with the best interests of the company, customers, and visitors in mind.

During business hours, all are expected to present a clean and neat appearance. Acceptable dress is defined by your immediate manager or supervisor within general guidelines.

People in management or sales positions are required to wear standard business suits or similar attire. Warehouse employees may wear casual slacks and shirts. Uniforms are provided for certain positions. Should your attire not comply with [YOUR COMPANY NAME] policy, you may be asked to go home and return in proper clothing without compensation for the time away from the office.

There are absolutely no exceptions to our personal appearance policy, and failure to comply may result in disciplinary action. Please direct any comments or questions regarding this policy to your immediate manager or supervisor or [*Person responsible for handling policy enforcement*]. Both are able to define in detail what constitutes acceptable and unacceptable attire. Thank you for helping [YOUR COMPANY NAME] maintain the highest professional image.

cc: [COPIES TO]

Personal Leave of Absence

TO: [*First and last name of person receiving memo*]

FROM: [YOUR NAME]
[YOUR TITLE]

DATE: [DATE]

SUBJECT: Leave of Absence Request for Personal Reason

No matter how rich a garden's soil may be, seeds must be sown and nutrients added to produce a harvest. The gardener meticulously and patiently cares for the crop as a mother cares for her child. Yet much to the gardener's chagrin, weeds still appear from time to time.

Whether for aesthetic or agricultural reasons, the undesirable is quickly removed from the rows of budding green. Life is a garden that blooms only when the right care and nutrients are applied. Unfortunately, we cannot rely on others to promote growth in our lives.

My personal garden needs attention right now. I prefer not to divulge the exact circumstances. Suffice it to say that I am embarrassed by the weeds that are affecting my growth and guilty that I have neglected my harvest.

If at all possible, I would like to take a personal leave from [*Date the leave begins*] through [*Date the leave ends*]. I realize it is a difficult approval in that I am keeping the reason confidential. [*First name of person receiving memo*], we have known each other for some time. You must trust me when I say I need to rebuild my garden now, not later. It is essential if there are to be any future crops. Please advise me of your decision as soon as possible, and thank you for understanding.

cc: [COPIES TO]

Personal Problems

TO: [*First and last name of person receiving memo*]

FROM: [YOUR NAME]
[YOUR TITLE]

DATE: [DATE]

SUBJECT: Apology

Occasionally, leaving our personal life at the door each morning on the way to work is hard. We are taught that professional performance requires a separation of business from home life. It's a good lesson and one I mistakenly believed had been perfected in my career.

Upon realizing that my personal life was affecting my work, I listed various ways to avoid similar situations in the future. The solution is simple. With an action plan in hand, I am confident that a dramatic change is imminent. Please accept my apologies for any concern I might have caused. I have recommitted myself to giving nothing less than 110% of myself to our company's success. You have my commitment from this day forward.

cc: [COPIES TO]

Personnel Information Changes

TO: All Staff

FROM: [YOUR NAME]
[YOUR TITLE]

DATE: [DATE]

SUBJECT: Personnel Information Changes

Had the renowned Sir Walter Raleigh received this memo, he would not have had much to reply. For 13 years, his contact and status information remained the same while he served time in prison.

Here at [YOUR COMPANY NAME], our records show that it's time again for you to update your personnel file. Please look over the following list and advise [*First and last name of person responsible for personnel files*] in writing of any changes that may have occurred by [*Date by which employees must submit changes*].

1. Home mailing address
2. Office and home telephone numbers
3. Cellular telephone number, if applicable
4. Names of all dependents
5. Emergency contacts
6. Educational accomplishments
7. Any civic and company awards

In addition to needing this information for the obvious contact reasons, management periodically reviews personnel files when jobs become available. Keeping personnel files up-to-date is the employee's ultimate responsibility. While you won't end up in prison if you don't provide the information, it is clearly in your best interest to do so.

cc: [COPIES TO]

Place Order for Supplies

[DATE]

[Mr./Mrs./Ms./Dr.] [FIRST AND LAST NAME]
[TITLE]
[COMPANY]
[ADDRESS]
[CITY], [STATE] [ZIP CODE]

Dear [Mr./Mrs./Ms./Dr.] [LAST NAME]:

New customers and increasing revenues enhance security for an entire company. It is important for every employee to realize that his or her individual actions contribute to everyone's welfare. I know [COMPANY]'s team knows the significance of maintaining customer satisfaction.

Therefore, I expect that professional attention will be given to our order for [*Name of product(s) ordered*]. [YOUR COMPANY NAME]'s decision was not made frivolously, as exhibited by the time required for our research. The price of $[*Dollar amount of price quoted for product(s) ordered*] is a bit high, but I believe additional value will ultimately be gained through consumer confidence.

I assume that you have specific requirements for payment and scheduling. Please contact me to discuss these in the immediate future. [*First name of person receiving letter*], I look forward to a long, professional relationship. Thank you for getting us off to a great start.

Sincerely yours,

[YOUR NAME]
[YOUR TITLE]

Pleasure to Work with Staff

[DATE]

[Mr./Mrs./Ms./Dr.] [CUSTOMER'S FULL NAME]
[CUSTOMER'S TITLE]
[COMPANY]
[ADDRESS]
[CITY], [STATE] [ZIP CODE]

Dear [Mr./Mrs./Ms./Dr.] [CUSTOMER'S LAST NAME]:

A crew is only as good as its captain. From shore to shore, the crew must be compelled and motivated to go beyond the call of duty for the captain, the ship, and themselves. Your crew's commitment to a tip-top ship is evident.

In my profession, I see many operations unlike [COMPANY] that are full of discontent and disregard for corporate goals. Seeing your staff truly teaming efforts in a pleasant atmosphere is my welcome mat for every visit. This says much about your leadership abilities.

I salute you, the captain, for your professionalism in creating an organization full of enthusiastic and talented people. Please accept my commendations and congratulations on your prosperity. With you at the helm, [COMPANY] is destined to be the best [*Describe the business focus of* COMPANY] from port to port.

Sincerely yours,

[YOUR NAME]
[YOUR TITLE]

Pleasure to Work with You

[DATE]

[Mr./Mrs./Ms./Dr.] [CUSTOMER'S FULL NAME]
[CUSTOMER'S TITLE]
[COMPANY]
[ADDRESS]
[CITY], [STATE] [ZIP CODE]

Dear [Mr./Mrs./Ms./Dr.] [CUSTOMER'S LAST NAME]:

Like any worthwhile relationship, a customer-vendor affiliation brings together ideas and common goals. Striking the delicate balance between likes and dislikes can sometimes be difficult. Two traits I hold in high regard personally and professionally are integrity and respect.

Consequently, I am compelled to tell you that working with you is an absolute pleasure. Everything is upbeat and up-front. Business is tough, but not with people like you.

Our relationship confirms that win-win situations occur when two people desire a positive result. Thank you for being a model customer. You make the reason I chose this profession obvious.

Sincerely yours,

[YOUR NAME]
[YOUR TITLE]

Positive PR Critique

[DATE]

[Mr./Mrs./Ms./Dr.] [FIRST AND LAST NAME]
[TITLE]
[COMPANY]
[ADDRESS]
[CITY], [STATE] [ZIP CODE]

Dear [Mr./Mrs./Ms./Dr.] [LAST NAME]:

Seeing your name in print along with the names of great leaders is an experience that defies complete description. There is the initial thrill, then disbelief, and finally an acknowledgment that perhaps you really are worthy of such an honor. I experienced a wide range of professional reinforcement reading the [*Date of publication*] issue of [COMPANY].

Of all the articles ever written about [YOUR COMPANY NAME], yours was one of the best. It conveyed the enthusiasm that suffuses our entire team. Writing is an art, and you have talents that should not be ignored or underestimated.

Yet, there is another feeling that came over me while reading the article. I had a successful business mentor once tell me quite bluntly, "Never believe your own press clippings." Now, many years after his death, these words come back to me as I realize how much further we have to go. [*First name of person receiving letter*], on behalf of [YOUR COMPANY NAME], thank you for a job well done.

Sincerely yours,

[YOUR NAME]
[YOUR TITLE]

Positive Response Adjustment

[DATE]

[Mr./Mrs./Ms./Dr.] [CUSTOMER'S FULL NAME]
[CUSTOMER'S TITLE]
[COMPANY]
[ADDRESS]
[CITY], [STATE] [ZIP CODE]

Dear [Mr./Mrs./Ms./Dr.] [CUSTOMER'S LAST NAME]:

No defense exists for a situation that jeopardizes customer satisfaction. Companies like [COMPANY] are [YOUR COMPANY NAME]'s link with prosperity. Thank you for apprising us of an error in [COMPANY]'s [*Describe the mistake*].

We have made an immediate change to reflect the correct [*Describe the area where the mistake was made*] as [*Describe* YOUR COMPANY NAME's *actions that fixed the mistake*]. Thank you for bringing this matter to our attention. [YOUR COMPANY NAME] always considers it beneficial when customers feel comfortable pointing out areas in which we fall below our high operational standards.

Sincerely yours,

[YOUR NAME]
[YOUR TITLE]

Press Release Verification

[DATE]

[Mr./Mrs./Ms./Dr.] [FIRST AND LAST NAME]
[TITLE]
[COMPANY]
[ADDRESS]
[CITY], [STATE] [ZIP CODE]

Dear [Mr./Mrs./Ms./Dr.] [LAST NAME]:

You have a tough job, and I do not want to make it any tougher. Everyone I know who is responsible for news tells me that they dislike receiving unsolicited telephone calls about press releases. Therefore, I promise that we will never call you unless you call us first.

We would like, however, to send you releases about our advances in [*Describe* YOUR COMPANY NAME's *main business emphasis*]. Please complete the following and return this letter to my attention in the enclosed self-addressed, stamped envelope.

____ Yes, you can send them by mail.
____ Yes, but instead of mailing, fax the releases to my office at
(______) _________-_______________.
____ No thank you, that isn't the news area I specialize in.

Thank you for helping us give you only the news you can use. We know your day is hectic enough keeping the public up to date.

Sincerely yours,

[YOUR NAME]
[YOUR TITLE]

Price Increase

[DATE]

[Mr./Mrs./Ms./Dr.] [CUSTOMER'S FULL NAME]
[CUSTOMER'S TITLE]
[COMPANY]
[ADDRESS]
[CITY], [STATE] [ZIP CODE]

Dear [Mr./Mrs./Ms./Dr.] [CUSTOMER'S LAST NAME]:

Would it help if I reminded you that these are inflationary times and the economy is tricky? Surely, [COMPANY] is feeling the pinch as much as [YOUR COMPANY NAME]. You know that, although sales may be increasing, profit margins are not keeping up.

In the past, we have done a fine job of shielding customers from economic concerns. Costs are rising at an unprecedented rate, however, leaving [YOUR COMPANY NAME] no alternative but to raise the price of [*Describe product/service with price increase*] by [*Dollar amount or percentage of price increase*].

Unlike other companies, we won't cut corners on product quality. [YOUR COMPANY NAME] never settles for second best, and we know you don't either. Thank you for understanding that this is not our choice; it is the economy's upper hand.

Sincerely yours,

[YOUR NAME]
[YOUR TITLE]

Price Increase Complaint

[DATE]

[Mr./Mrs./Ms./Dr.] [FIRST AND LAST NAME]
[TITLE]
[COMPANY]
[ADDRESS]
[CITY], [STATE] [ZIP CODE]

Dear [Mr./Mrs./Ms./Dr.] [LAST NAME]:

Anger results from disappointment. We believe that if the roles were reversed, the actions taken would not have been our own. Pardon my anger over receiving notification that [COMPANY] has increased the price dramatically for [*Describe product or service*].

I find it inconceivable, however, that [COMPANY]'s management could have approved such a ludicrous move. You are forcing many established customers, like [YOUR COMPANY NAME], to look elsewhere. [COMPANY] is not the only company selling [*Describe product or service*]. My professional career has formed around solid relationships and ours appears to be ending.

This is precisely why I have chosen to vent my disappointment through this letter. Up to now, I chose [COMPANY]. Your professional practices were quite respectable and consistent with our own. As this is no longer the case, know that we are evaluating other sources for our needs.

To stop other vendor proposals from entering my office, [COMPANY] must fulfill its customer satisfaction obligations and live up to our company's expectations. If this is possible, please telephone at your earliest convenience. I hope to hear from you shortly. Your price increase is a dangerous and losing proposition, but together we can change its direction.

Sincerely yours,

[YOUR NAME]
[YOUR TITLE]

Price Not as Quoted

[DATE]

[Mr./Mrs./Ms./Dr.] [FIRST AND LAST NAME]
[TITLE]
[COMPANY]
[ADDRESS]
[CITY], [STATE] [ZIP CODE]

Dear [Mr./Mrs./Ms./Dr.] [LAST NAME]:

From conglomerates to neighborhood shops, companies are required by law to represent products and pricing accurately. Falsifying advertisements or product claims either blatantly or in small print is not well-received. Consumer advocate groups work with government agencies to enforce truth in advertising.

On [*Date*], [YOUR COMPANY NAME] purchased [*Describe and list by number with believed price what* YOUR COMPANY NAME *purchased from* COMPANY] from [COMPANY] based solely on the representations found in [*Publication showing lower price for what* YOUR COMPANY NAME *purchased from* COMPANY], where it clearly states that the price is $[*Dollar amount of price advertised for*].

[YOUR COMPANY NAME] was charged $[*Dollar amount of price paid for listed items purchased from* COMPANY], resulting in an overpayment of $[*Dollar amount*]. I presume that this is merely an oversight on [COMPANY]'s part. I harbor no harsh thoughts, but I do expect a refund in the immediate future. Thank you for your prompt attention and reply.

Sincerely yours,

[YOUR NAME]
[YOUR TITLE]

Problem Not Under Warranty

[DATE]

[Mr./Mrs./Ms./Dr.] [CUSTOMER'S FULL NAME]
[CUSTOMER'S TITLE]
[COMPANY]
[ADDRESS]
[CITY], [STATE] [ZIP CODE]

Dear [Mr./Mrs./Ms./Dr.] [CUSTOMER'S LAST NAME]:

Be it in a community, personal, or professional situation, rules meet and create challenges simultaneously. In providing direction, they are not always universally accepted, but rules are an indispensable part of life.

Upon hearing of your problem with [*Name of product needing repair*], I spent the better part of today going over our policies and looking for a way to get around our warranty procedures. I know how conscientious you are, and I anticipated your questions. You probably read our warranty coverage agreement and realized that the required repairs on [*Name of product needing repair*] fall outside the provisions of the agreement.

Unfortunately, I could not uncover a way to abate the estimated repair cost of $[*Dollar amount of repair for item or product needing repair*]. At times like this, I wish I could bend the rules for a valuable customer like [COMPANY]. We will get started immediately after receiving your telephone call authorizing the necessary repairs. Thank you for your understanding in this matter.

Sincerely yours,

[YOUR NAME]
[YOUR TITLE]

Product Replacement Offered

[DATE]

[Mr./Mrs./Ms./Dr.] [CUSTOMER'S FULL NAME]
[CUSTOMER'S TITLE]
[COMPANY]
[ADDRESS]
[CITY], [STATE] [ZIP CODE]

Dear [Mr./Mrs./Ms./Dr.] [CUSTOMER'S LAST NAME]:

Surprises have no place in business. Whether a handshake or a contract seals a deal, unanticipated events lower credibility. Once that's gone, the odds of a beneficial affiliation are slim.

[YOUR COMPANY NAME] takes pride in being the most trusted name in the [*Describe* YOUR COMPANY NAME's *major business emphasis*] business. Therefore, any order requiring product substitution is handled promptly and directly. We wouldn't want you to think you ordered X and were mistakenly sent Y.

[*Describe what the order was for*], recently ordered by [COMPANY], is currently unavailable. However, [*Describe the replacement*], which we recommend as a substitute, has been very well received by customers. The price difference of $[*Dollar amount of price difference between what the order was for and the replacement*] can be handled by [*Actions* COMPANY *should take to receive the replacement*]. While we are confident that you will find [*Describe the replacement*] acceptable, we require your confirmation before shipping. Just call [*Telephone number at* YOUR COMPANY NAME *to handle replacement*], and we'll handle the rest. This way when your order arrives, there won't be any surprises.

Sincerely yours,

[YOUR NAME]
[YOUR TITLE]

Program Cancelled

TO: [*First and last name of person receiving memo*]

FROM: [YOUR NAME]
[YOUR TITLE]

DATE: [DATE]

SUBJECT: Benefits Program Canceled

Employers and employees are partners in the truest sense. The good of the organization is dependent on the good of the individual contributors. Believing this, [YOUR COMPANY NAME] willingly carries tremendous responsibilities in assuming the roles of caretaker and provider for our employees and their families.

Notifying our colleagues of unfortunate news is a difficult task. Still, increasing costs during economically troubled times have prohibited the continuation of [YOUR COMPANY NAME]'s benefits program. We have no alternative but to recommend private coverage incurred at each employee's expense.

For more information on alternative benefit plans, please contact [*First and last name of person responsible for benefits program*]. Thank you for understanding that we had no choice in this matter. [YOUR COMPANY NAME] hopes to resume companywide benefits programs for our employees when the economic tide turns.

cc: [COPIES TO]

Project Support

TO: [*First and last name of person receiving memo*]

FROM: [YOUR NAME]
[YOUR TITLE]

DATE: [DATE]

SUBJECT: Thank You

Professional accomplishment is not the result of a single day's work. Carefully considered actions build upon one another until the goal is achieved. Look at any successful person, and it will be evident that he or she did not get there alone.

Achievers acknowledge areas of inadequacy and are not afraid to obtain qualified assistance in reaching their goals. The key is finding a complementary personality who is also compelled to be the best in his or her chosen field. I take this time to say that I found a match while working with you on [*Name of project*].

You were such an instrumental member of the team, assisting the project by [*Describe contributions of person receiving memo*]. Please know that your dedication and hard work are appreciated, and I look forward to our next opportunity to work together. Thank you again for sharing the expertise that helped bring [*Name of project*] to a positive conclusion.

cc: [COPIES TO]

Promotion of Employee

TO: [*First and last name of person receiving memo*]

FROM: [YOUR NAME]
[YOUR TITLE]

DATE: [DATE]

SUBJECT: Congratulations on Your Promotion

Success is a journey the destination of which changes frequently. From city to city, we walk many paths in search of fulfillment. Lessons get tucked neatly into our pack, and we see other travelers on the same route charting their own futures.

Ambition and motivation separate leaders from followers. Achievement changes the path's direction. The character you have shown in leading your group, often carrying more than your load, is appreciated by [YOUR COMPANY NAME]. It is my pleasure to acknowledge your accomplishments by promoting you to [*Title of new position of person receiving memo*] effective [*Date the promotion takes effect*].

Besides a more distinguished title, this position carries additional compensation and responsibilities. These will be explained by your new manager, [*First and last name of promoted's new manager*], soon. You will not need a map to chart your career path at [YOUR COMPANY NAME]; a successful journey is in store. The entire management team thanks you for your participation in our future. We value you as one of our leaders.

cc: [COPIES TO]

Prompt Payment

[DATE]

[Mr./Mrs./Ms./Dr.] [CUSTOMER'S FULL NAME]
[CUSTOMER'S TITLE]
[COMPANY]
[ADDRESS]
[CITY], [STATE] [ZIP CODE]

Dear [Mr./Mrs./Ms./Dr.] [CUSTOMER'S LAST NAME]:

If we hang around long enough, trends make a complete circle. While the 90s offered fast-track promises, the 21st century has seen an upsurge in conservative ideals. As ethics and integrity assume renewed importance, promptness has also taken on increased significance.

Whether in internal or external company endeavors, we know that consistent and dependable actions inspire confidence. To have this reciprocated by our customers through prompt payments is the highest honor. It leads us to believe that the conservative ideals on which not only [YOUR COMPANY NAME], but our great nation, were founded are appreciated by [COMPANY].

Thank you for upholding admirable principles at a time when so many have become lax in observing the tenets that past generations esteemed most.

Sincerely yours,

[YOUR NAME]
[YOUR TITLE]

Proxy Vote

[DATE]

[Mr./Mrs./Ms./Dr.] [FIRST AND LAST NAME]
[TITLE]
[COMPANY]
[ADDRESS]
[CITY], [STATE] [ZIP CODE]

Dear [Mr./Mrs./Ms./Dr.] [LAST NAME]:

The vision of democracy set forth by our founding fathers endures today in the opportunity to voice opinions by casting votes. Preservation of freedom is our responsibility, and I hope that you, as a [YOUR COMPANY NAME] stockholder, do not take it lightly. Although you are unable to attend our Annual Meeting on [*Date of Annual Meeting*], you can still voice your opinion with this proxy statement.

Please appoint [YOUR COMPANY NAME]'s Corporate Secretary as your representative and complete the following:

This vote covers [*Describe the issue voted on*].

_______ I VOTE FOR
_______ I VOTE AGAINST

____
Signature

____
Printed Name

____
Date

It is imperative that this document be received before the Annual Meeting on [*Date of Annual Meeting*]. Thank you for your voice and participation in [YOUR COMPANY NAME]'s future directions.

Sincerely yours,

[YOUR NAME]
[YOUR TITLE]

Purchase Offer

[DATE]

[Mr./Mrs./Ms./Dr.] [FIRST AND LAST NAME]
[TITLE]
[COMPANY]
[ADDRESS]
[CITY], [STATE] [ZIP CODE]

Dear [Mr./Mrs./Ms./Dr.] [LAST NAME]:

An equitable deal goes beyond the immediate benefits to the two parties signing a contract. The business world is small, and we cross paths with our associates again and again. [YOUR COMPANY NAME]'s goal in a negotiation is to ensure that when, and if, that happens our ethics will be remembered favorably.

In a clearly win-win proposition, we hereby submit an offer to purchase from [COMPANY] the following: [*Describe and list by number of what* YOUR COMPANY NAME *wants to purchase from* COMPANY]. It is understood the payment for said purchase will be made in the form of [*Describe the manner in which* YOUR COMPANY NAME *is going to pay* COMPANY *for the item to be purchased from* COMPANY] totaling $[*Dollar amount* YOUR COMPANY NAME *is going to pay* COMPANY *for the purchase from* COMPANY], which includes all past, present, and future interests in, ownership of, and titles to [*Describe and list by number of what* YOUR COMPANY NAME *wants to purchase from* COMPANY].

We reserve the right to review particular [*Describe and list by number of what* YOUR COMPANY NAME *wants to purchase from* COMPANY] documentation and financial data prior to completing the purchase. [YOUR COMPANY NAME] stands by its commitment to making the present our future. I look forward to receiving [COMPANY]'s positive response to our offer.

Sincerely yours,

[YOUR NAME]
[YOUR TITLE]

Quoted

[DATE]

[Mr./Mrs./Ms./Dr.] [CUSTOMER'S FULL NAME]
[CUSTOMER'S TITLE]
[COMPANY]
[ADDRESS]
[CITY], [STATE] [ZIP CODE]

Dear [Mr./Mrs./Ms./Dr.] [CUSTOMER'S LAST NAME]:

Eloquence and speech are not the same. Expressing one's ideas is easy; expressing them with style requires forethought. Please do not think your insightful quotation on [*Describe the subject of the quotation*] in [*Name of publication in which the quotation appeared*] went unnoticed.

On the contrary, your discerning vision left readers with a well-founded reference point. Congratulations on being recognized for your expertise. I hope to be reading your name more often. Your eloquence is rare and admirable; it reflects the confidence and knowledge reserved for people with a winning attitude. We have enough chatter in our lives.

Sincerely yours,

[YOUR NAME]
[YOUR TITLE]

Received Company Award

[DATE]

[Mr./Mrs./Ms./Dr.] [CUSTOMER'S FULL NAME]
[CUSTOMER'S TITLE]
[COMPANY]
[ADDRESS]
[CITY], [STATE] [ZIP CODE]

Dear [Mr./Mrs./Ms./Dr.] [CUSTOMER'S LAST NAME]:

The demands of our chosen professions often exhaust us as we strive to create opportunities from challenges. The personal satisfaction found in a job done well, however, prepares us for the next goal.

Outside professional recognition and respect are equally important. I am pleased to hear that [COMPANY] has honored your achievements with its prestigious [*Name of* COMPANY's *award*] award. It really could not be bestowed on a more deserving recipient. Management and peer appreciation of your unrelenting efforts to [*Describe why person receiving letter got* COMPANY's *award*] must give you a great sense of satisfaction.

Congratulations on a well-earned tribute; I extend my best wishes for continued success and additional trophies.

Sincerely yours,

[YOUR NAME]
[YOUR TITLE]

Recognition

TO: [*First and last name of person receiving memo*]

FROM: [YOUR NAME]
[YOUR TITLE]

DATE: [DATE]

SUBJECT: Thank You

The greater the accomplishment, the greater the significance of receiving acknowledgment from those held in esteem. Since we first worked together, I have admired and respected your judgment and decision-making ability. Frankly, these are both areas I have been working on myself.

The reinforcement of my efforts by a person I hold in high regard is appreciated. Thank you for the positive feedback regarding my contribution to [*Describe what you did that the person receiving memo recognized*]. With the additional confidence gained from this accomplishment and your recognition, I feel ready to take on new responsibilities and meet new challenges.

cc: [COPIES TO]

Referred to Another

[DATE]

[Mr./Mrs./Ms./Dr.] [CUSTOMER'S FULL NAME]
[CUSTOMER'S TITLE]
[COMPANY]
[ADDRESS]
[CITY], [STATE] [ZIP CODE]

Dear [Mr./Mrs./Ms./Dr.] [CUSTOMER'S LAST NAME]:

In the 1930s, 30 cents created and mailed a letter. This cost has risen to nearly $18 over the last 60 years. The hidden and obvious costs of sending a letter add up quickly.

Not the least of these costs is the time of the person who writes the letter. Thank you for taking the time to inform [YOUR COMPANY NAME] of your recent displeasure concerning [*Describe* COMPANY's *complaint*].

Like most organizations, [YOUR COMPANY NAME] is divided by responsibilities. Addressing your situation properly requires expert handling by someone more qualified than I. I have briefed [*First and last name of person handling the complaint*] on the situation and left our meeting confident that your complaint is in good hands.

Thank you again for writing and letting us know that [YOUR COMPANY NAME] failed to live up to the expectations of [COMPANY]. With [*First and last name of person handling the complaint*] on your side, your next letter will surely be one of praise.

Sincerely yours,

[YOUR NAME]
[YOUR TITLE]

Refund for Damaged Goods

[DATE]

[Mr./Mrs./Ms./Dr.] [CUSTOMER'S FULL NAME]
[CUSTOMER'S TITLE]
[COMPANY]
[ADDRESS]
[CITY], [STATE] [ZIP CODE]

Dear [Mr./Mrs./Ms./Dr.] [CUSTOMER'S LAST NAME]:

Every spring and summer, workers the world over pick fruits and vegetables. Great care is given to selecting only the best quality from the crop. Then, when the produce arrives in the market, consumers' hands put it to still another test, choosing only those fruits and vegetables that have survived the trip from the orchard or field in good condition.

[YOUR COMPANY NAME] prides itself on maintaining the highest total quality management controls. It's so rare for a bruised apple to pass by the inspector and make its way into a customer's order that frankly, I am appalled. Therefore, I have enclosed a complete refund in the amount of $[*Dollar amount of refund*].

In our [*Number of years* YOUR COMPANY NAME *has been in business*] years of doing business, we have planted the seeds season after season to ensure bountiful crops. Please accept our apologies for an order that was less than what we both strive for, that is, the best for our respective companies and families.

Sincerely yours,

[YOUR NAME]
[YOUR TITLE]

Refusal of Credit

[DATE]

[Mr./Mrs./Ms./Dr.] [CUSTOMER'S FULL NAME]
[CUSTOMER'S TITLE]
[COMPANY]
[ADDRESS]
[CITY], [STATE] [ZIP CODE]

Dear [Mr./Mrs./Ms./Dr.] [CUSTOMER'S LAST NAME]:

Saying no to a customer is not easy, but [YOUR COMPANY NAME]'s formal guidelines governing credit extensions must be followed to maintain equitable treatment for all our customers.

Unfortunately, we cannot comply with [COMPANY]'s request for credit. [YOUR COMPANY NAME] does its best to promote, not inhibit, business affiliations. If you believe there has been an error or omission in the information provided on your credit application, please bring this to our immediate attention. We may be able to reverse our decision.

The application can be reprocessed here in the office without starting from scratch. [YOUR COMPANY NAME] appreciates your understanding that our company is committed to service. Please feel free to reapply in another [*Length of time before* COMPANY *can reapply for credit*] months. Today, based on the information we have in hand, we have no choice in the matter.

Sincerely yours,

[YOUR NAME]
[YOUR TITLE]

Rejection of Goods

[DATE]

[Mr./Mrs./Ms./Dr.] [FIRST AND LAST NAME]
[TITLE]
[COMPANY]
[ADDRESS]
[CITY], [STATE] [ZIP CODE]

Dear [Mr./Mrs./Ms./Dr.] [LAST NAME]:

Many companies fear the judicial system's increasing interference in commercial enterprise. Yet, there is no reason for apprehension when business practices are fair and in compliance with existing agreements. Much to our dismay, [YOUR COMPANY NAME] has been forced to question [COMPANY]'s adherence to oral and written commitments.

[YOUR COMPANY NAME]'s recent order of [*Description of product rejected*] does not conform to the representations made by [COMPANY]. As clearly stated within [COMPANY]'s [*Document containing description rejected product information*]. [*Description of product rejected*] was to be as presented in [*Document containing description of product rejected's product information*]. The contradictions are obvious to anyone who so much as glances at [*Description of product rejected*] and [*Document containing description of product rejected information*].

Therefore, we have no choice but to reject, and return, [*Description of product rejected*] for a full refund in the amount of $[*Dollar amount paid for product rejected*]. I suggest that [COMPANY] investigates the displeasure caused by this unfortunate situation. It may yield results that will benefit future customer relationships.

Sincerely yours,

[YOUR NAME]
[YOUR TITLE]

Renewal

[DATE]

[Mr./Mrs./Ms./Dr.] [CUSTOMER'S FULL NAME]
[CUSTOMER'S TITLE]
[COMPANY]
[ADDRESS]
[CITY], [STATE] [ZIP CODE]

Dear [Mr./Mrs./Ms./Dr.] [CUSTOMER'S LAST NAME]:

Doesn't it seem like the days move quicker as we get older? Count it in the strange but true category that the time has come for us to renew our contract for [*Describe contract's purpose*] with [COMPANY]. We have enjoyed doing business with your company and need concurrence on our future dealings.

To prevent any interruption in service, please sign page [*Page number of contract* COMPANY *must sign*] and then return the entire document to my attention at your earliest convenience. The entire [YOUR COMPANY NAME] staff thanks you in advance for your continued business. Before the coming days turn quickly into weeks, we ask you to follow Benjamin Franklin's advice, "Don't put off until tomorrow what you can do today!"

Sincerely yours,

[YOUR NAME]
[YOUR TITLE]

Request

[DATE]

[Mr./Mrs./Ms./Dr.] [CUSTOMER'S FULL NAME]
[CUSTOMER'S TITLE]
[COMPANY]
[ADDRESS]
[CITY], [STATE] [ZIP CODE]

Dear [Mr./Mrs./Ms./Dr.] [CUSTOMER'S LAST NAME]:

Each of us is the product of our experiences. We travel different routes that mold who we are and what we become. No matter where we have been, I believe we all have something to contribute to others' lives.

While my name may be foreign to you, our language is the same and our backgrounds are similar. I have traveled highways that have taken me into businesses just like [COMPANY]; I have experiences that you can learn from. My record shows a strong commitment to keeping customers ahead in the race for success.

In one short meeting, I would like to show you a map that could put [COMPANY] on the road to cost containment and prosperity. I hope you accept the phone call that will open new channels of information.

Sincerely yours,

[YOUR NAME]
[YOUR TITLE]

Request for Product Demonstration

[DATE]

[Mr./Mrs./Ms./Dr.] [FIRST AND LAST NAME]
[TITLE]
[COMPANY]
[ADDRESS]
[CITY], [STATE] [ZIP CODE]

Dear [Mr./Mrs./Ms./Dr.] [LAST NAME]:

Surveys suggest that people use about 10 percent of total purchases after six to twelve months of having the goods. This fact is easy to understand when we consider how quickly situations change and how inclined we are to impulse buying.

To limit [YOUR COMPANY NAME]'s participation in this statistic, we would like some hands-on time with [COMPANY]'s [*Name of product*]. [*Name of* COMPANY's *employee or documentation*] presented the product's features well, and at first glance, it appears that the product would be beneficial to our operation. Yet, a [*Number of days* YOUR COMPANY NAME *wants to evaluate the product*]-day, no-obligation, evaluation period would solidify our purchasing decision.

In addition to increasing our customer satisfaction level, granting the above request serves [COMPANY]'s purposes too. [YOUR COMPANY NAME]'s decision would be made during the trial period. Additional marketing efforts would be unnecessary, and [YOUR COMPANY NAME] would be less likely to return [*Name of product*] after purchase.

Be assured that our entire staff will treat [*Name of product*] as if it were our own, that is, with extreme care. I look forward to hearing your plan to provide [*Name of product*] for [YOUR COMPANY NAME]'s evaluation. Today's economy does not grant us the luxury of keeping 90 percent of our purchases in the closet.

Sincerely yours,

[YOUR NAME]
[YOUR TITLE]

Request for References

[DATE]

[Mr./Mrs./Ms./Dr.] [FIRST AND LAST NAME]
[ADDRESS]
[CITY], [STATE] [ZIP CODE]

Dear [Mr./Mrs./Ms./Dr.] [LAST NAME]:

Protocols define accepted practices. Incorporating the standard phrase "References provided upon request" in a resume is a common practice. Although we have spent only a brief time together, you have probably noticed [YOUR COMPANY NAME]'s rigorous attention to detail. Our success demands maintenance of high standards.

Your credentials and presentation impressed me, so I would now like to take the next step in the hiring process, which calls for requesting references from three business associates.

Please forward by [*Date* YOUR COMPANY NAME *wants references by*] a list to my attention that contains the following information for each reference: complete mail and telephone contact information, beginning date of affiliation with you, and a brief paragraph describing your relationship.

I, or a member of my staff, will contact some or all of your references before our next meeting. Thank you for fulfilling your resume's written commitment. I look forward to confirming my belief in your future with [YOUR COMPANY NAME].

Sincerely yours,

[YOUR NAME]
[YOUR TITLE]

Request for Resumé

[DATE]

[Mr./Mrs./Ms./Dr.] [FIRST AND LAST NAME]
[TITLE]
[COMPANY]
[ADDRESS]
[CITY], [STATE] [ZIP CODE]

Dear [Mr./Mrs./Ms./Dr.] [LAST NAME]:

From time to time, you hear of a person who possesses a certain successful air—a person who is admired and stands above the crowd in his or her chosen profession. [YOUR COMPANY NAME] looks for such presence and knowledge in our managers and employees.

I write with the hope that you are in a position to explore career alternatives. From what I know, we could be the company that precisely matches your short- and long-term goals. I am interested in receiving your professional profile or resumé if you are interested in a potential career move to [YOUR COMPANY NAME] as our newest [*Title of position available*].

Timing is very important in life and I understand my initiative may not come at a convenient time. Nevertheless, I would appreciate a reply. Thank you for advising me of your thoughts in the matter. It is hard to find good people like you.

Sincerely yours,

[YOUR NAME]
[YOUR TITLE]

Request Not Acknowledged

[DATE]

[Mr./Mrs./Ms./Dr.] [FIRST AND LAST NAME]
[TITLE]
[COMPANY]
[ADDRESS]
[CITY], [STATE] [ZIP CODE]

Dear [Mr./Mrs./Ms./Dr.] [LAST NAME]:

I understand that many professionals feel like puppets subject to the whims of customers, management, and suppliers. Everyone seems to want something often at the most inopportune time. While I empathize, I still wonder why [YOUR COMPANY NAME]'s recent request for [*Subject of request*] has not been acknowledged by [COMPANY].

We handle our customer requests immediately to maintain high operating and satisfaction standards. As previously outlined, we are seeking [*Describe and list by number what* YOUR COMPANY NAME *wants from* COMPANY]. Given proper attention, this would seem to be a relatively easy task.

Please take a break from the puppet show and fulfill our request. I look forward to receiving [COMPANY]'s reply or, at the very least, an update on the status of our request. Thank you for your assistance in the matter.

Sincerely yours,

[YOUR NAME]
[YOUR TITLE]

Request to Complete Forms

TO: [*First and last name of person receiving memo*]

FROM: [YOUR NAME]
[YOUR TITLE]

DATE: [DATE]

SUBJECT: Benefit Forms Completion Request

It has been surmised that if the copy machine had been invented before World War II, no one would have won the conflict. Paper, rather than soldiers, would have filled the bunkers. While paperwork can be irritating, it is often the best mode of communication.

The time is here to complete benefits forms for [*Year the benefits forms cover*], and unfortunately, there is no better way than in writing. You do not have to participate in the program; we provide benefits because [YOUR COMPANY NAME] is committed to improving the lives of its employees.

Take a moment to read the instructions that will help you complete the forms accurately and thoroughly. A little extra effort now simplifies information processing later. And this way, we can cut down just a bit on the paperwork for everyone.

cc: [COPIES TO]

Resignation Notice

TO: [*First and last name of person receiving memo*]

FROM: [YOUR NAME]
[YOUR TITLE]

DATE: [DATE]

SUBJECT: Resignation Notice

Professional growth is inspiring and isolating simultaneously. While accomplishments are gratifying, the achievement drives us beyond our previous expectations. Standards are raised for the next challenge, and separation from the familiar increases.

In my life, I have learned to seize challenge whenever it crosses my path. I try always to approach my quest for success with zeal. We are truly the ultimate creators of our destinies.

Unfortunately, my professional goals are no longer compatible with those of my position as [*Title of position leaving*]. This warrants a change in direction and focus. After much deliberation, I believe the time has come for me to move forward without [YOUR COMPANY NAME]. I hereby respectfully submit my resignation and provide [*Time in weeks of resignation notice*] weeks' notice.

I thank you and [YOUR COMPANY NAME] for an unparalleled opportunity to grow, which has allowed me to prepare for my next challenge. [*First name of person receiving memo*], you have been an inspiration to me, and I hope we can keep abreast of each other's successes.

cc: [COPIES TO]

Response To

TO: [*First and last name of person receiving memo*]

FROM: [YOUR NAME]
[YOUR TITLE]

DATE: [DATE]

SUBJECT: Thank you

Acknowledgment of another's efforts in today's fast-paced business environment is often overlooked. It means a great deal to have the appreciation of those you admire. This is especially true for a person like me to whom a career is more than an occupation.

Your recognition of the efforts I put forth to [*One or two words describing accomplishment*] reinforces my opinion that we are truly a team here at [YOUR COMPANY NAME]. I could not have done it alone, and your guidance continues to compel me to be the best player possible. Every pennant winner needs a coach directing his or her moves, and I could not have a better one.

Thank you for all you have done for my career and for taking the time to let me know that I am a valuable member of our team. I hold your opinion in the highest regard.

cc: [COPIES TO]

Restrictions Placed on Credit

[DATE]

[Mr./Mrs./Ms./Dr.] [CUSTOMER'S FULL NAME]
[CUSTOMER'S TITLE]
[COMPANY]
[ADDRESS]
[CITY], [STATE] [ZIP CODE]

Dear [Mr./Mrs./Ms./Dr.] [CUSTOMER'S LAST NAME]:

Business rulebooks are necessary to fair play. [YOUR COMPANY NAME]'s credit policies are applicable to new and existing customers without exception. Besides the terms and conditions governing payments, established guidelines extend into other areas.

One rule requires credit limitations when a customer's account indicates [*Describe problem causing restriction*]. Therefore, [COMPANY]'s account is restricted in the following manner: [*Describe restriction*]. To resume normal credit allowances, [*Describe how to remove restriction*] must occur by [*Date to remove restriction must happen by*].

We appreciate your immediate attention in rectifying the situation and for understanding that rules benefit everyone. Thank you for your professionalism in this very important matter. Please remember, customer satisfaction is important to me, and I will help in any way possible.

Sincerely yours,

[YOUR NAME]
[YOUR TITLE]

Results Outline

[DATE]

[Mr./Mrs./Ms./Dr.] [CUSTOMER'S FULL NAME]
[CUSTOMER'S TITLE]
[COMPANY]
[ADDRESS]
[CITY], [STATE] [ZIP CODE]

Dear [Mr./Mrs./Ms./Dr.] [CUSTOMER'S LAST NAME]:

When ideas are exchanged freely, different interpretations are a likely result. This seems especially true in dynamic and thought-provoking meetings like the one we had on [Date of meeting]. At times, I found myself not taking notes for fear of missing the next comment.

My understanding of our discussion regarding [*Topic of meeting*] is as follows: [*Describe the results of the meeting*].

I want to feel confident that we came away from the meeting with the same conclusions. Take a look and let me know if you see anything that might lead us in the wrong direction. Thank you in advance for the feedback.

Sincerely yours,

[YOUR NAME]
[YOUR TITLE]

Resumé Handling Policy

TO: [*First and last name of person receiving memo*]

FROM: [YOUR NAME]
[YOUR TITLE]

DATE: [DATE]

SUBJECT: Resumé Handling Policy

Government statistics confirm that finding suitable employment is a trying task. There are many highly qualified people competing for a relatively small number of openings. Because [YOUR COMPANY NAME] is renowned as a reputable organization, we receive many resumes from prospective candidates without any recruitment efforts.

All resumes, whether for an internal job change or a new opening, must be submitted to [*Name of person or department responsible for resumés*]. [*Name of person or department responsible for resumés*] serves as the central point of contact, administering the interview and selection process. Following [*Pronoun referring to person receiving memo's gender, i.e., "his" or "her"*] review and preliminary reference check, management is given a list of prospective candidates with which to begin the interview process.

Regulations require [YOUR COMPANY NAME] to hold all resumés for [*Length of time resumes are held on file by* YOUR COMPANY NAME]. Therefore, your compliance with this policy is mandatory. Thank you for your assistance in ensuring that all candidates are treated equitably.

cc: [COPIES TO]

Resumé Response

[DATE]

[Mr./Mrs./Ms./Dr.] [FIRST AND LAST NAME]
[TITLE]
[COMPANY]
[ADDRESS]
[CITY], [STATE] [ZIP CODE]

Dear [Mr./Mrs./Ms./Dr.] [LAST NAME]:

The reputation as a desirable employer is the highest honor the professional community can bestow on a company. [YOUR COMPANY NAME] considers our team family, and the strictest guidelines are followed regarding indoctrination of new members. Because of these rules, career and company developments have caused many to seek success within our walls.

Choosing the few we will call when openings exist is a trying process. With so many qualified people competing for the same positions, resumés are reviewed only when jobs are available. Be assured, however, that yours was received and that we will be in contact when your skills match our company needs.

If for some reason our paths do not cross during the next six months, please send us an updated resumé reflecting any recent accomplishments or changes in contact information. Thank you for your interest in [YOUR COMPANY NAME]. We consider it significant that you took the time to introduce yourself to us.

Sincerely yours,

[YOUR NAME]
[YOUR TITLE]

Retirement

TO: [*First and last name of person receiving memo*]

FROM: [YOUR NAME]
[YOUR TITLE]

DATE: [DATE]

SUBJECT: Your Retirement

Youth holds the most splendid of gifts—our dreams. As we travel the country roads and city highways of life, we turn these visions into realities. Along the way, we give of ourselves continually in return for rewards.

I am envious of you as you embark upon a new stage in your life—a stage that will allow you to appreciate the scenery along the road. No longer will you be tied to the duties and responsibilities that obscure the view. Strange isn't it, that it takes a lifetime to achieve the ultimate freedom of action, thought, and sight?

Now you have time to pursue all the dormant desires life's pressures did not allow you to investigate. I'd like to hear all about the roadside cafés we passed by on our journey because we didn't have the time to stop. Let's meet for coffee at one someday soon.

cc: [COPIES TO]

Retirement of Employee

TO: All Staff

FROM: [YOUR NAME]
[YOUR TITLE]

DATE: [DATE]

SUBJECT: Never-To-Be-Forgotten [*First and last name of person retiring*] Is Retiring

It's going to be difficult not seeing [*First and last name of person retiring*]'s face each day. For [*Number of years employed*] years, [*Pronoun referring to retired person's gender, i.e., "he" or "she," "him" or "her"*] has been pursuing new challenges with fierce determination. [*First name of person retiring*] has been a valuable addition to our company. To say simply we'll miss [*Pronoun referring to retired person's gender, i.e., "him" or "her"*] is an understatement.

Still, [*Pronoun referring to retired person's gender, i.e., "he" or "she,"*] is saying good-bye to us for a world without pressure, fixed routines, or pending deadlines. Let's all extend our warmest congratulations and wishes to [*First name of person retiring*] for much health and happiness in the years ahead.

cc: [COPIES TO]

Safety Reminder

TO: [*First and last name of person receiving memo*]

FROM: [YOUR NAME]
[YOUR TITLE]

DATE: [DATE]

SUBJECT: Safety Reminder

In the 10 seconds it took you to read this far, an accident probably happened in our community because someone did not observe safety precautions. [YOUR COMPANY NAME] has an established safety awareness program that is a top priority for the entire work force.

I remind you that its success depends on everyone taking responsibility for safe work practices and procedures. One wrong move could endanger yourself and others. Exercising caution protects all employees, customers, and visitors.

Some of the safety guidelines developed within the awareness program are as follows: [*Describe safety guidelines needing reinforcement*]. Equipment operation and safety manuals are located [*Location of the equipment operation and safety manuals in office*]. Still, the best safety recommendations come from the people closest to the program.

I encourage our employees to advise [*First and last name of person responsible for enforcing safety rules*] of any unsafe conditions or suggestions for improving safety in our company. [*Pronoun referring to the person responsible for enforcing safety rules's gender, i.e., "He" or "She"*] is dedicated to administering and monitoring [YOUR COMPANY NAME]'s safety awareness program and can be reached at [*Telephone number of person responsible for enforcing safety rules*]. Thank you for taking the extra time to practice safety in your work area.

cc: [COPIES TO]

Salary Increase Request

TO: [*First and last name of person receiving memo*]

FROM: [YOUR NAME]
[YOUR TITLE]

DATE: [DATE]

SUBJECT: Compensation Increase Request

Asking for a raise is a difficult task. I've been writing this memorandum in my head for some time, trying to find the words that will reaffirm my value to [YOUR COMPANY NAME]. I wanted first to draw attention one-by-one to my accomplishments and the daily responsibilities benefiting our team in both the short- and the long term.

Next, there would be a gentle reminder that my salary has not been increased for [*Length of time since last salary increase*]. Inflation continues to increase, and money does not go as far as it once did. And finally, I would close with a standard request for a reevaluation of my total compensation package, trusting that my value as an employee and team member would be reflected in a well-deserved increase.

After further deliberation, I decided that this approach was not necessary, because as an effective coach, you stay close to your players. You are very familiar with my work habits and my dedication to the company. You would want to be fair and reward my efforts.

If you prefer, I can still write the memorandum originally planned. The first few paragraphs would be different; the ending the same. I believe my compensation increase request of [*Dollar amount or percentage increase requested*] is reasonable. If the request is not approved, I would like your help in formulating an action plan designed to help me obtain the increase in the very near future. Thank you in advance for acknowledging my value to [YOUR COMPANY NAME].

cc: [COPIES TO]

Sales Referral

[DATE]

[Mr./Mrs./Ms./Dr.] [CUSTOMER'S FULL NAME]
[CUSTOMER'S TITLE]
[COMPANY]
[ADDRESS]
[CITY], [STATE] [ZIP CODE]

Dear [Mr./Mrs./Ms./Dr.] [CUSTOMER'S LAST NAME]:

In politics, private opinions influence public polls. Individual judgments based on experiences, education, and environment combine to produce the will of the masses on election day. Contrary to popular belief, one person's individual vote can affect the outcome of a political candidate's campaign.

I appreciate your personal endorsement and vote of confidence in my career as demonstrated in your referral of [*Name of company that* COMPANY *told to call you*] as a prospective customer. This fine example of private opinion going public serves to reinforce my stand on professional issues. I will let you know how my first meeting with [*Name of company that* COMPANY *told to call you*] at the "primary" turns out. Thank you for casting your vote in the right direction.

Sincerely yours,

[YOUR NAME]
[YOUR TITLE]

SBA Request

[DATE]

[Mr./Mrs./Ms./Dr.] [FIRST AND LAST NAME]
[TITLE]
[COMPANY]
[ADDRESS]
[CITY], [STATE] [ZIP CODE]

Dear [Mr./Mrs./Ms./Dr.] [LAST NAME]:

Where would America be without the determined few who seek to fulfill their dreams? Innovation and progress are not possible without futurists who visualize change and then make it happen. For years, the Small Business Administration (SBA) has assisted dreamers with practical professional support.

I provide an abstract of our fledgling organization with a special request. Apparently, your position demands knowledge of SBA operations that I could only hope to achieve. Because of your expertise, I ask you to read the following and make any suggestions you think we might find useful.

Briefly, [YOUR COMPANY NAME] is on the verge of an exciting venture to provide [*Describe* YOUR COMPANY NAME's *main business emphasis*]. Our company founders are [*Ethnic origin of all* YOUR COMPANY NAME's *founders*], [*Race of all* YOUR COMPANY NAME's *founders*], and [*Gender of all* YOUR COMPANY NAME's *founders*], which may, or may not, place us in categories for which government sponsored grants and/or loans are available. Please forward to my attention any applications and materials that may be beneficial. Thanks for your professionalism. We cannot achieve our dream without your assistance and SBA support.

Sincerely yours,

[YOUR NAME]
[YOUR TITLE]

Security

TO: [*First and last name of person receiving memo*]

FROM: [YOUR NAME]
[YOUR TITLE]

DATE: [DATE]

SUBJECT: Security Reminder

Security is of utmost importance, both at home and in the workplace. The precautions we take protect us from harm. [YOUR COMPANY NAME] enforces security measures covering both information and property for the good of our employees, customers, and visitors.

[YOUR COMPANY NAME]'s security program requires the cooperation of our entire team of professionals. I remind you that no one is exempt from the rules we have developed to keep the workplace secure. They must be followed by all to serve all.

Briefly, our security program prohibits [*Describe security guidelines needing reinforcement*]. In accordance with the law, inspections of office furniture may be conducted from time to time with or without your notice. Confidential information should be disposed of by [*Describe the manner in which you want employees to dispose of confidential information*]. It should be stored in [*Describe the manner in which you want employees to store confidential information*].

If you have any comments or questions regarding [YOUR COMPANY NAME]'s security policy, contact [*First and last name of person responsible for enforcing security rules*] at [*Telephone number and first and last name of person responsible for enforcing security rules*]. [*Pronoun referring to person responsible for enforcing security rules's gender, i.e., "He" or "She"*] is available to review our security program upon request. Thank you for your continued protection of our environment, information, and property.

cc: [COPIES TO]

Seminar Announcement

[DATE]

[Mr./Mrs./Ms./Dr.] [CUSTOMER'S FULL NAME]
[CUSTOMER'S TITLE]
[COMPANY]
[ADDRESS]
[CITY], [STATE] [ZIP CODE]

Dear [Mr./Mrs./Ms./Dr.] [CUSTOMER'S LAST NAME]:

Do we ever reach a point in our lives when there is nothing new to learn? Absolutely not; we do, indeed, learn something new every day. Although [*Topic of the seminar*]'s story is not a complete secret, a wide range of fallacies and facts have been described in articles, advertisements, and rumors.

Having the right information is key to decision making. To provide this, we are hosting an exciting seminar on [*Date of the seminar*] from [*Time seminar begins*] to [*Time seminar ends*] at [*Location of seminar*]. Any person interested in [*Topic of the seminar*] must learn how to distinguish the valid from the unsubstantiated claims.

Although the seminar carries a $[*Price of seminar*] charge, one cannot put a price on intellectual power. Rather than simply reading about [*Topic of the seminar*], take the first step today to increase your knowledge. Call [*Telephone number to reserve a seat at seminar*] and reserve your place among the decision makers who want the facts. You'll be glad you did.

Sincerely yours,

[YOUR NAME]
[YOUR TITLE]

Send-off Letter

[DATE]

To whom it may concern:

Skillful pilots gain a reputation maneuvering machines through both tranquil weather conditions and raging thunderstorms. Each situation requires a different approach, but a successful landing is always the ultimate goal. Employees like [*First and last name of employee*] enable organizations to manage traffic patterns with professional skill.

It always gives me great pleasure to copilot, direct and manage a successful person's moves. Recently, I had such an experience when [*First and last name of employee*] made important contributions to [YOUR COMPANY NAME] from [*Starting date of employee's employment with* YOUR COMPANY NAME] through [*Ending date of employee's employment with* YOUR COMPANY NAME]. [*Pronoun referring to employee's gender, i.e., "his" or "her"*] achievements included [*Describe and list by number employee's successes*].

I can recommend [*Pronoun referring to employee's gender, i.e., "his" or "her"*] knowledge, skills, and talents heartily. Beyond being achievement-oriented and enthusiastic, [*Pronoun referring to employee's gender, i.e., "he" or "she"*] has the ability to get the job done. Any company that hires [*First and last name of employee*] will defy gravity and successfully land time after time, no matter what the weather.

Sincerely yours,

[YOUR NAME]
[YOUR TITLE]

Sexual and Other Discrimination

TO: [*First and last name of person receiving memo*]

FROM: [YOUR NAME]
[YOUR TITLE]

DATE: [DATE]

SUBJECT: Sexual and Other Unlawful Discrimination and Harassment

Whether favoritism or discrimination, prejudice is an enemy of a free people. [YOUR COMPANY NAME] does not tolerate any form of discrimination, harassment, or prejudice in our internal or external business affairs.

[YOUR COMPANY NAME] is committed to providing its employees a work environment free of actions, comments, jokes, or words based on a person's age, ethnicity, race, religion, sex, or any other characteristic legally protected. Either blatant or implied, sexual and other forms of unlawful discrimination and harassment are among the worst kinds of employee misconduct and, as such, are strictly prohibited.

Any incident of possible sexual or other unlawful discrimination or harassment should be reported immediately to your manager or supervisor. If you believe this is inappropriate, contact [*Person responsible for handling policy enforcement*]. Be assured that your report will be held in the strictest confidence, and have no fear of reprisal. Managers and supervisors must immediately report any incident of sexual or other unlawful discrimination or harassment.

Please direct any comments or questions regarding this policy to your immediate manager or supervisor or to [*Person responsible for handling policy enforcement*]. There are absolutely no exceptions to [YOUR COMPANY NAME]'s policy governing the prohibition of any sexual or other unlawful discrimination or harassment. Any employee misconduct of this type will be subject to disciplinary action that may lead to termination of employment. Thank you in advance for your total support of this policy.

cc: [COPIES TO]

Shipping Error Apology

[DATE]

[Mr./Mrs./Ms./Dr.] [CUSTOMER'S FULL NAME]
[CUSTOMER'S TITLE]
[COMPANY]
[ADDRESS]
[CITY], [STATE] [ZIP CODE]

Dear [Mr./Mrs./Ms./Dr.] [CUSTOMER'S LAST NAME]:

Quality is the responsibility of every member of the organization. Long before [YOUR COMPANY NAME]'s shipping department ever emerged, management developed a comprehensive quality assurance handbook. The overriding goal is customer satisfaction from start to finish.

Shipping department training takes place regularly. As our business expands, additional employees are assimilated into the system. Frankly, they were doing a good job shipping customer orders until, on one specific day last [*Time from when error occurred to when this letter is sent, i.e., "week" or "month"*], a few forgot the handbook's cast-in-stone quality assurance lessons.

Error crept in. Unfortunately, our records show that [COMPANY] was shipped [*Describe merchandise received by* COMPANY] in place of the requested [*Describe merchandise requested by* COMPANY]. I would like to make the merchandise exchange with the least inconvenience to [COMPANY]. Therefore, I propose [*Describe how* YOUR COMPANY NAME *wants to exchange merchandise received by* COMPANY *for merchandise requested by* COMPANY]. Please let me know if this is convenient for you. Thank you for your patience and understanding. We have taken steps to prevent this distressing incident from recurring.

Sincerely yours,

[YOUR NAME]
[YOUR TITLE]

Signed Contract Transmittal

[DATE]

[Mr./Mrs./Ms./Dr.] [FIRST AND LAST NAME]
[TITLE]
[COMPANY]
[ADDRESS]
[CITY], [STATE] [ZIP CODE]

Dear [Mr./Mrs./Ms./Dr.] [LAST NAME]:

Making a mutually beneficial business deal requires a great deal of time and effort. Thank you for the professionalism that has resulted in the agreement between [YOUR COMPANY NAME] and [COMPANY]. The executed contracts for [*Describe and list by number the contract's purposes*], signed by [*First and last name of person who signed contract*], are enclosed.

After verifying that all [*Total number of pages in contract*] pages have been received, please retain the document for your files. [YOUR COMPANY NAME] looks forward to a long and prosperous relationship with [COMPANY] under the terms and conditions of the contract. Again, my thanks for your assistance. We could not have gotten this far without your support.

Sincerely yours,

[YOUR NAME]
[YOUR TITLE]

Smoking Policy

TO: [*First and last name of person receiving memo*]

FROM: [YOUR NAME]
[YOUR TITLE]

DATE: [DATE]

SUBJECT: Smoking Policy

[YOUR COMPANY NAME] company policy entitles every employee to a clean and healthy work environment. Pollutant-free air helps create surroundings in which we can strive for individual and corporate success. [YOUR COMPANY NAME]'s smoking policy is to be followed without exception.

In accordance with state and local laws, smoking is prohibited in [*Location where smoking is prohibited in office*] excluding designated smoking areas. At [YOUR COMPANY NAME], the designated smoking area is [*Location of designated smoking area in office*]. Failure to comply with this policy may result in disciplinary action.

There are absolutely no exceptions to our smoking policy, and failure to comply may result in disciplinary action. Please direct any comments or questions regarding this policy to your immediate manager or supervisor. Thank you in advance for your assistance in maintaining [YOUR COMPANY NAME]'s clean and healthy work environment.

cc: [COPIES TO]

Smoking Warning

TO: [*First and last name of person receiving memo*]

FROM: [YOUR NAME]
[YOUR TITLE]

DATE: [DATE]

SUBJECT: Clean Air Benefits Everyone

Despite the warnings printed on every pack of cigarettes sold in the United States, millions of people knowingly risk their health. We know cigarette smoking causes cancer in smokers. We know second-hand smoke is detrimental to nonsmokers too.

To guarantee the best work environment for every [YOUR COMPANY NAME] employee, we have policies that must be followed without exception. One of these is our smoking policy. Among other things, the policy clearly states, "Smoking is prohibited in all public areas excluding designated smoking areas." Here at [YOUR COMPANY NAME], the designated smoking area is [*Place where designated smoking area is located*].

Take this note as a friendly reminder that your compliance is obligatory. If you have any questions, please do not hesitate to let me know. Thank you for your support of a healthy work environment for all to enjoy.

cc: [COPIES TO]

Speaker Confirmation

[DATE]

[Mr./Mrs./Ms./Dr.] [FIRST AND LAST NAME]
[TITLE]
[COMPANY]
[ADDRESS]
[CITY], [STATE] [ZIP CODE]

Dear [Mr./Mrs./Ms./Dr.] [LAST NAME]:

Based on the tremendous response, our audience knows your reputation for engaging and entertaining, knowledge-filled presentations, so we look forward to filling the room with your voice and people eager to learn about [*Topic of speech*].

As a confirmation, [YOUR COMPANY NAME]'s conference is on [*Date of conference*] at [*Location of conference*] beginning at [*Time conference starts*]. Your speech is scheduled from [*Time person receiving letter starts speech*] to [*Time person receiving letter ends speech*]. Let me know if you need any special equipment such as a projector or VCR. I am confident that your involvement will help make this our most successful and enlightening event yet.

Sincerely yours,

[YOUR NAME]
[YOUR TITLE]

Speaker Discount Fee Request

[DATE]

[Mr./Mrs./Ms./Dr.] [FIRST AND LAST NAME]
[TITLE]
[COMPANY]
[ADDRESS]
[CITY], [STATE] [ZIP CODE]

Dear [Mr./Mrs./Ms./Dr.] [LAST NAME]:

Asking an audacious question of an admired person is uncomfortable. The biggest risk is offending the person and disrupting what could have been a business opportunity. There are times when it does hurt to ask.

I have given considerable thought to the predicament I now face. To say that we are merely impressed with your professional profile is an understatement. Your breadth of experience has sparked a sincere interest in confirming your attendance at [*Name of conference*] on [*Date of conference*].

Our staff has spent hours reworking the budget trying to find the funds for your standard fee. Frankly, no matter how many times the bottom line is erased, a positive number never appears. Pardon me for asking, but is there any way your fee could be reduced? Could you speak for a shorter time? Could we pay your expenses?

Please do not take our request as an insult; [YOUR COMPANY NAME] respects your talents immensely. We hope to reach a compromise so our audience can benefit from your experience. Let me know if you are still interested. Hopefully, I will hear from you soon.

Sincerely yours,

[YOUR NAME]
[YOUR TITLE]

Speaker Outline Request

[DATE]

[Mr./Mrs./Ms./Dr.] [FIRST AND LAST NAME]
[TITLE]
[COMPANY]
[ADDRESS]
[CITY], [STATE] [ZIP CODE]

Dear [Mr./Mrs./Ms./Dr.] [LAST NAME]:

Fulfilling people's expectations can be a real challenge. When launching a seminar, much thought is given to the background and knowledge of the audience. Our goal with [*Name of conference*] on [*Date of conference*] is to provide such a fulfilling experience that each person walks away confident that the time could not have been better spent.

The decision committee has reviewed your impressive professional speaking credentials. From the overview, it appears that we may have an exact fit between your expertise and our expectations. However, we need just a little more information before reaching a decision.

An outline detailing and highlighting specific points you might cover would be helpful. If at all possible, please ensure delivery to my attention before the committee's next meeting on [*Date outline is required*]. Thank you in advance for your help in enabling us to make our decision in the most efficient manner. People with your outstanding credentials are few and far between.

Sincerely yours,

[YOUR NAME]
[YOUR TITLE]

Speaker Slide Copy Request

[DATE]

[Mr./Mrs./Ms./Dr.] [FIRST AND LAST NAME]
[TITLE]
[COMPANY]
[ADDRESS]
[CITY], [STATE] [ZIP CODE]

Dear [Mr./Mrs./Ms./Dr.] [LAST NAME]:

Applause is just fleeting recognition of a good job. After the crowds have left and the auditorium is silent, professionals move on to the next achievement with added confidence and higher expectations. The applause for your impressive display of knowledge at our [*Name of conference*] on [*Date of conference*] still echoes.

The comments and evaluations gathered from your audience were outstanding. In fact, several members have requested copies of your slides.

If possible, please forward one original set to my attention. I will deliver copies to the people who request them. Thank you for a very informative, professional presentation. I look forward to revisiting the topics myself through the slides.

Sincerely yours,

[YOUR NAME]
[YOUR TITLE]

Stockholder's Annual Earnings

[DATE]

[Mr./Mrs./Ms./Dr.] [FIRST AND LAST NAME]
[TITLE]
[COMPANY]
[ADDRESS]
[CITY], [STATE] [ZIP CODE]

Dear [Mr./Mrs./Ms./Dr.] [LAST NAME]:

With each ending, there is a beginning. Identifying accomplishments within time-based constraints provides knowledge that can influence future directions. As this [*Time the earnings reflect, i.e., "quarter" or "year"*] draws to a close, I report that [YOUR COMPANY NAME]'s financial results clearly indicate the attainment of past objectives.

Propelled by our executive team's commitment to success, steady progress was reported in all operational areas. In summary, net sales were $[*Dollar amount of net sales for time the earnings reflect, i.e., "quarter" or "year"*] reflecting a [*Percentage of decrease or increase as compared to previous time the earnings reflect, i.e., "quarter" or "year"*] percent [*Movement of percentage of decrease or increase as compared to previous time the earnings reflect, i.e., "quarter" or "year"; i.e., "decrease" or "increase"*] due to [*Describe reason(s) for percentage of decrease or increase as compared to previous time the earnings reflect, i.e., "quarter" or "year"; i.e., "decrease" or "increase"*]. The attached statements provide a detailed analysis of [YOUR COMPANY NAME]'s financial profile.

Increasing market presence and new developments promise financial growth. I take this opportunity to pay tribute to our loyal employees and stockholders for their dedication. Together, we have the knowledge, skills, and talents we need to approach the coming [*Time the earnings reflect, i.e., "quarter" or "year"*] confident in our continued prosperity.

Sincerely yours,

[YOUR NAME]
[YOUR TITLE]

Stockholder's Annual Report

[DATE]

[Mr./Mrs./Ms./Dr.] [FIRST AND LAST NAME]
[TITLE]
[COMPANY]
[ADDRESS]
[CITY], [STATE] [ZIP CODE]

Dear [Mr./Mrs./Ms./Dr.] [LAST NAME]:

There is much more to a company's success than earnings ratios. The numbers are simply a by-product of the time and effort expended taking a proactive stance in this dynamic marketplace. [YOUR COMPANY NAME]'s most valuable asset is not inscribed on our balance sheet; it is the teamwork of knowledgeable and talented people dedicated to excellence.

Last year was both challenging and exciting. We progressed steadily toward achieving our goal to [*Describe the most important goal achieved*]. These accomplishments facilitated maturation and growth, enabling the implementation of plans that include [*Describe and list by number future goals based on the most important goal achieved's completion*]. All of these actions enhance the value of our company.

Even in a highly competitive marketplace and uncertain economy, we controlled variables resulting in [*Provide financial overview*]. Our financial future holds endless possibilities as advancements lead to success. On behalf of [YOUR COMPANY NAME], I thank you for your support as we approach the next year together, confident in our company's imminent prosperity.

Sincerely yours,

[YOUR NAME]
[YOUR TITLE]

Stronger Reminder

[DATE]

[Mr./Mrs./Ms./Dr.] [CUSTOMER'S FULL NAME]
[CUSTOMER'S TITLE]
[COMPANY]
[ADDRESS]
[CITY], [STATE] [ZIP CODE]

Dear [Mr./Mrs./Ms./Dr.] [CUSTOMER'S LAST NAME]:

Time is money. Unfortunately, we have been wasting much of both in trying to collect [COMPANY]'s debt to [YOUR COMPANY NAME]. In every management meeting, we discuss with disbelief the fact that [COMPANY] continues to shirk its obligations. The outstanding balance of $[*Dollar amount of payment needed from* COMPANY] is overdue by an excessive [*Length of time amount of payment needed from* COMPANY *is past due*].

I am responsible for our company's accounting, and your lack of action has forced me to cancel all future extensions of credit. Because [YOUR COMPANY NAME] is a fair company, management has developed two options that will allow [COMPANY] to fulfill its obligations:

1. Remit the full amount of $[*Dollar amount of payment needed from* COMPANY]; or
2. Remit a partial payment of $[*Dollar amount of partial payment needed from* COMPANY] with the understanding that the balance is to be paid by [*Date dollar amount of partial payment needed from* COMPANY *is due*].

If given the opportunity, I will help [COMPANY]. Your immediate response is imperative. [YOUR COMPANY NAME] is not going away, and I would like our business affiliation to continue. However, only your actions can allow this to happen, and time is running out.

Sincerely yours,

[YOUR NAME]
[YOUR TITLE]

Substance Abuse

TO: [*First and last name of person receiving memo*]

FROM: [YOUR NAME]
[YOUR TITLE]

DATE: [DATE]

SUBJECT: I Care About You

Strength has nothing to do with one's physical prowess. It is reflected, rather, in the way in which a person survives difficult times. Hardships can result in only one of two things.

They either elevate us to a higher level or deplete our resources until weakness overshadows hope. It takes a strong person to put aside pride and recognize potential problem areas in life. A weak person gives in to the persuasive power of substances that allow different feelings or not at all.

Frankly, I worry about the changes I have noticed in your behavior and work patterns, because they are typical of people who are abusing [*One or two words defining the substance name of person receiving memo is abusing*]. I fear that unless the situation is corrected immediately, I will lose a valuable employee and team member. You are not alone, and I want to help you get on the right track again. We all need assistance in our lives at one point or another.

The ultimate decision to bring back the person you once were belongs to you and no one else. Only you can take the difficult first step—acknowledging that a problem exists. I would like to set up a completely confidential meeting with a professional familiar with [*One or two words defining the substance name of person receiving memo is abusing*] problems. A strong person acknowledges situations that may be too much to handle alone; strength increases with another's help. And, this is not a weakness.

cc: [COPIES TO]

Summary of Meeting

TO: [*First and last name of person receiving memo*]

FROM: [YOUR NAME]
[YOUR TITLE]

DATE: [DATE]

SUBJECT: [*One or two words defining meeting's purpose]* Meeting Summary

Diligence leads to accomplishment. A cooperative focus on goals, as recently exhibited in our meeting pertaining to [*One or two words defining meeting's purpose*], definitely promotes attainment. In the course of that discussion, areas were revealed requiring a review of the facts to ensure that our future directions are complementary.

Therefore, the following is a summary of the meeting on [*Date the meeting was held*]. While a memo alone cannot do the discussion justice, my interpretation of the conclusions drawn and actions required is as follows: [*Describe up to five points covered in meeting*].

When you have had a chance to review this summary, I would welcome your comments. We need to move forward as quickly as possible. Thank you for your continued support in upholding our goals and completing our mission. Your recommendations will be given serious consideration.

cc: [COPIES TO]

Telephone Use Policy

TO: [*First and last name of person receiving memo*]

FROM: [YOUR NAME]
[YOUR TITLE]

DATE: [DATE]

SUBJECT: Telephone Use Policy

Like most organizations, [YOUR COMPANY NAME] has gone to great lengths to ensure that employees have the tools they need as they pursue company goals. Telephones are provided to employees to use in conducting company business and should not be used for personal calls.

A personal telephone call is defined as a communication made on, or with, company equipment that is not directly related to your job. This includes local and long distance calls. While local calls are not limited, some job responsibilities require a long distance access code to place calls outside the immediate dialing area.

Long distance access codes are assigned at the discretion of your manager or supervisor. There are absolutely no exceptions to our telephone policy, and failure to comply may result in disciplinary action.

Please direct any comments or questions regarding this policy to your immediate manager or supervisor. Thank you in advance for your support of [YOUR COMPANY NAME]'s policies.

cc: [COPIES TO]

Temporary Agency Inquiry

[DATE]

[Mr./Mrs./Ms./Dr.] [FIRST AND LAST NAME]
[TITLE]
[COMPANY]
[ADDRESS]
[CITY], [STATE] [ZIP CODE]

Dear [Mr./Mrs./Ms./Dr.] [LAST NAME]:

As it parallels the economic product life cycle model, a business moves through many stages of development. Controlling progress is essential to the success of any company. If progress is not kept under control, the business may suffer decline or, even worse, demise.

Although [YOUR COMPANY NAME] is prospering, budgetary constraints do not guarantee another employee long-term stability. Caught in the precarious position of needing assistance, we seek a temporary worker to join our team of professionals as a [*Name of position open by* COMPANY].

This person should be available [*Number of hours worked per week in position open by* COMPANY] hours per week starting on [*Date the person for the position open by* COMPANY *should begin work*]. The following skills are necessary: [*Describe and list by number skills needed to perform the duties of the position open*]. I anticipate that this person will be with our company for [*Length of time* YOUR COMPANY NAME *needs the position open by* COMPANY].

Please forward any [COMPANY] contracts, forms, and professional referrals to my attention. While I am positive that [COMPANY] performs extensive screening, [YOUR COMPANY NAME] requests three candidate interviews before choosing our new "employee." Thank you for the assistance that will enable us to continue growing strong.

Sincerely yours,

[YOUR NAME]
[YOUR TITLE]

Terminating the Agency

[DATE]

[Mr./Mrs./Ms./Dr.] [FIRST AND LAST NAME]
[TITLE]
[COMPANY]
[ADDRESS]
[CITY], [STATE] [ZIP CODE]

Dear [Mr./Mrs./Ms./Dr.] [LAST NAME]:

It's unfortunate when any business relationship comes to an unanticipated ending. Yet, there are times when the reasons to separate outweigh any justification we may have to join forces. [YOUR COMPANY NAME] has given serious consideration to the question of whether our best interest continues to be served by retaining [COMPANY]'s advertising services.

After evaluating the costs versus the results, management has decided to terminate our relationship with your firm effective [*Date relationship with* COMPANY *ends*]. This letter serves as formal notification that [YOUR COMPANY NAME] no longer requires your assistance. Please close out our account, cancel any pending media placements, and forward the final invoice to [*First and last name of person in* YOUR COMPANY NAME *responsible for invoices*]'s attention.

Thank you for your professional handling of this matter. Time brings about change, and the world is a very small place. Perhaps we will have a chance to work together in the future when circumstances are different.

Sincerely yours,

[YOUR NAME]
[YOUR TITLE]

Termination Notice

TO: [*First and last name of person receiving memo*]

FROM: [YOUR NAME]
[YOUR TITLE]

DATE: [DATE]

SUBJECT: Termination Notice

Misadventures teach many of life's most valuable lessons. When faced with an unfavorable situation, it is best to reflect upon the actions that created the problem. There is never only one action or party totally in the wrong.

We have the opportunity to learn from our errors. For every action, there is an equal and opposite reaction. Although [YOUR COMPANY NAME] has repeatedly made you aware that a change was needed in [*Describe why first and last name of person receiving memo's employment is being terminated*], no improvement has been apparent over the last [*Time lapse between when first and last name of person receiving memo was informed of the problem and when terminated*].

Your lack of action leaves us no choice but to terminate your employment with [YOUR COMPANY NAME] effective [*Date the employment termination takes effect*].

Your future outside [YOUR COMPANY NAME] is dependent upon your recognizing that we are not alone in finding behavior of this type unacceptable. Learn from your mistakes, and there is a chance you can have all you ever dreamed of.

cc: [COPIES TO]

Termination of Contract

[DATE]

[Mr./Mrs./Ms./Dr.] [FIRST AND LAST NAME]
[TITLE]
[COMPANY]
[ADDRESS]
[CITY], [STATE] [ZIP CODE]

Dear [Mr./Mrs./Ms./Dr.] [LAST NAME]:

The letter serves as official notice that the [*Name of the agreement*] agreement, dated [*Date* YOUR COMPANY NAME *and* COMPANY *signed the agreement*], by and between [YOUR COMPANY NAME] and [COMPANY], shall be hereby considered terminated effective on [*Date the contract is terminated*]. Therefore, as of [*Date the contract is terminated*] we are no longer bound or obligated to fulfill any terms and conditions contained within [*Name of the agreement*] here and as above described.

I have enclosed a duplicate copy of this Termination of Contract notice for your signature to acknowledge receipt of this letter. Please return one signed original to my attention. If there are any questions, please do hesitate to contact me. Thank you in advance for your prompt attention.

Sincerely yours,

[YOUR NAME]
[YOUR TITLE]

Agreed and Consented by:
[COMPANY]

____

Signature

____

Printed Name and Title

____

Date

Termination V

TO: [*First and last name of person receiving m*

FROM: [YOUR NAME]
[YOUR TITLE]

DATE: [DATE]

SUBJECT: Termination Warning Requires Immediate Action

It takes time to figure out our direction in life. We may try our hands at several things before settling on one career pursuit that makes us eager to start the new day. For some time, I have been questioning whether [YOUR COMPANY NAME] does this for you as it does for me.

On many occasions, we have discussed the problem with your performance in the area of [*Describe reason(s) performance is unacceptable*]. I made it perfectly clear that [YOUR COMPANY NAME] wants you to succeed and to continue being a member of our team. To do this, you must change your performance immediately by [*Describe recommendations for improved performance*].

Should you continue to neglect this area and not show any reasonable improvement, I will be forced to take stronger measures. Please be advised that your employment with [YOUR COMPANY NAME] is in jeopardy. Unless your performance improves by [*Date by which improved performance must occur*], I will recommend proceedings that may lead to your immediate termination. [*First name of person receiving memo*], heed this warning by showing me that your career at [YOUR COMPANY NAME] is important to you. I really would like you to stay.

cc: [COPIES TO]

Territory Change

TO: [*First and last name of person receiving memo*]

FROM: [YOUR NAME]
[YOUR TITLE]

DATE: [DATE]

SUBJECT: Territory Change and Realignment

No prospering business can remain static in today's changing environment. Our sales force, which represents a large segment of our operation, is directly influenced by these changes. Occasionally, territory assignments must be realigned in response to industry and market conditions.

We have given the highest priority to promoting individual opportunities for achievement. When allocating resources, previous success and sales focus are weighed along with potential for growth. Please note the following changes in your territory assignment effective [*Date territory change is effective*].

Your new territory consists of [*Describe new territory*]. A list of sales in process and not yet closed from your previous assignment must be presented to me in writing by [*Date by which first and last name of person receiving memo should advise you of any sales from old territory assignment*]. The status of these accounts will be determined on a case-by-case basis using established criteria.

If you have any comments or questions, bring these to my attention immediately. I extend my wishes for continued success in this new assignment.

cc: [COPIES TO]

Thank You

[DATE]

[Mr./Mrs./Ms./Dr.] [CUSTOMER'S FULL NAME]
[CUSTOMER'S TITLE]
[COMPANY]
[ADDRESS]
[CITY], [STATE] [ZIP CODE]

Dear [Mr./Mrs./Ms./Dr.] [CUSTOMER'S LAST NAME]:

There is a big difference between market intelligence and market research. Getting the facts through market research is only half the job; market intelligence is putting them to good use. Thank you for giving us the whole picture as we continually strive to evaluate and improve our performance.

Your cooperation and participation in our recent customer survey yielded valuable insight. We do not underestimate the value of the objective views shared by [COMPANY]. Frankly, your honesty helps us improve our operations for all of our customers.

There appears to be no limit to either intelligence or ignorance in our lives; either can make or break any situation. Thank you again for your assistance in helping us grow smarter.

Sincerely yours,

[YOUR NAME]
[YOUR TITLE]

Thank You for Assistance

[DATE]

[Mr./Mrs./Ms./Dr.] [FIRST AND LAST NAME]
[TITLE]
[COMPANY]
[ADDRESS]
[CITY], [STATE] [ZIP CODE]

Dear [Mr./Mrs./Ms./Dr.] [LAST NAME]:

In this competitive business world, an unselfish helping hand is rare indeed. Fighting the tendency to self-absorption is difficult as pressures escalate. Yet, there is much gratification in knowing that your actions were beneficial to another's life.

Because of your assistance, I was able to [*Describe results from assistance*]. While it's up to me now, the initial results would not have been possible without your support. [*First name of person receiving letter*], thank you for making me more aware of ways in which I can help others and for reaffirming my belief in the goodness of human nature.

Sincerely yours,

[YOUR NAME]
[YOUR TITLE]

Thank You for Endorsement

[DATE]

[Mr./Mrs./Ms./Dr.] [FIRST AND LAST NAME]
[TITLE]
[COMPANY]
[ADDRESS]
[CITY], [STATE] [ZIP CODE]

Dear [Mr./Mrs./Ms./Dr.] [LAST NAME]:

Turning aspirations into realities is easier when quality people are supportive of your efforts. Thank you for sharing your knowledge and time with me as I worked on [*Describe the subject of endorsement*]. Our conversation is with me still as I transcribe mental notes in preparation for the future.

It was reassuring to know that a person like you shared my vision. I am putting your recommendations into action and am confident that the results will be positive. I extend my utmost appreciation and thanks for your professional endorsement. You really have had an influence on my life.

Respectfully yours,

[YOUR NAME]
[YOUR TITLE]

Thank You for Meeting

[DATE]

[Mr./Mrs./Ms./Dr.] [FIRST AND LAST NAME]
[TITLE]
[COMPANY]
[ADDRESS]
[CITY], [STATE] [ZIP CODE]

Dear [Mr./Mrs./Ms./Dr.] [LAST NAME]:

It has been estimated there are more than 200,000 useless words in the English language. Many times, conversations are full of them; they waste our time and accomplish nothing. Our meeting today was exceptional in that we were able to achieve much without wasting time on gibberish.

I found your breadth of experience and apparent knowledge enlightening. There are many avenues for us to pursue based on our mutual interests. Because of this, I propose [*Describe and list by number actions resulting from meeting*]. Thank you for taking time out of your busy schedule. I look forward to seeing you again and sharing another engaging conversation.

Sincerely yours,

[YOUR NAME]
[YOUR TITLE]

Thank You for Referral

[DATE]

[Mr./Mrs./Ms./Dr.] [FIRST AND LAST NAME]
[TITLE]
[COMPANY]
[ADDRESS]
[CITY], [STATE] [ZIP CODE]

Dear [Mr./Mrs./Ms./Dr.] [LAST NAME]:

Many of the best telephone calls we receive start with, "I was referred to you by ..." Knowing that someone believes in us reinforces our ideals and goals. Thank you for initiating [*First and last name of person referred*]'s interest in [YOUR COMPANY NAME] for a potential business affiliation.

I realize that much more than time is involved in making a referral. Your reputation as a credible source is on the line too. Be assured that I will treat [*First name of person referred*] with the utmost respect. Again, thank you for the referral, and when the opportunity arises, please know I will return your gracious extension of support.

Sincerely yours,

[YOUR NAME]
[YOUR TITLE]

Theft Insurance Claim

[DATE]

[Mr./Mrs./Ms./Dr.] [FIRST AND LAST NAME]
[TITLE]
[COMPANY]
[ADDRESS]
[CITY], [STATE] [ZIP CODE]

Dear [Mr./Mrs./Ms./Dr.] [LAST NAME]:

The days of unlocked doors and front porch communities are long gone. Crime continues to pervade our nation, as the overpopulated prisons attest. I have learned that it really does not matter how secure your environment is anymore.

When a criminal wants to steal, he or she finds a way. On [*Date theft occurred*] at approximately [*Time theft occurred*], [YOUR COMPANY NAME] was victimized by theft. A police report was filed, and the criminal [*As relates to arrest of thief, "has" or "has not"*] been apprehended. A partial list of the property discovered missing is as follows: [*Describe and list by number missing items*].

Because our [COMPANY] insurance policy, number [YOUR COMPANY NAME's *insurance policy number assigned by* COMPANY], covers theft, I hope to recoup our losses as soon as possible. Let me know how I can help you get the job done. Thank you for your professional assistance leading to a speedy settlement. It's a terrible shame that the illicit acts of a few force the rest of us to imprison ourselves within our environments.

Sincerely yours,

[YOUR NAME]
[YOUR TITLE]

Time is Open Request

TO: [*First and last name of person receiving memo*]

FROM: [YOUR NAME]
[YOUR TITLE]

DATE: [DATE]

SUBJECT: [*One or two words defining meeting*] Meeting Request

Knowledge lessens the potential for error in business ventures. Especially when a goal's critical point is approaching, detailing efforts expended thus far with a person of experience yields practical results. This is precisely the reason I would like to consult with you about [*One or two words defining meeting*].

By most indications, we are on track. However, I believe that your valuable input will increase the likelihood of a positive outcome. Specifically, the areas I seek your opinion on are [*Describe up to five separate meeting points to cover*].

I understand that your time is limited, so I will adjust my schedule to accommodate yours. Thank you in advance for your assistance in ensuring this project's success. Although this is not an emergency situation, I hope to confer with you at your earliest convenience.

cc: [COPIES TO]

Time is Running Out

[DATE]

[Mr./Mrs./Ms./Dr.] [CUSTOMER'S FULL NAME]
[CUSTOMER'S TITLE]
[COMPANY]
[ADDRESS]
[CITY], [STATE] [ZIP CODE]

Dear [Mr./Mrs./Ms./Dr.] [CUSTOMER'S LAST NAME]:

Have you ever really thought about a fruit? Even with artificial light and stimulants, fruit ripens at its own pace. All the efforts of modern science have failed to shorten significantly the growth cycle of a shiny red apple.

We have planted the seeds, watched our business relationship grow, and now the time has arrived for you to reap the harvest. Our fruit is ready for picking. Fruit selected at the wrong time is not of the highest grade.

Left too long in the market, it perishes. Management advised me recently that [COMPANY]'s decision is crucial. I fear time is running out and our prime offer for [*Describe what the deal is for and terms*] will soon have been on the tree too long. The fruit is available to everyone, but obviously, I want [COMPANY] to have first choice. Please let me know what I can do to help you act quickly. It would be a shame for you to miss this golden opportunity.

Sincerely yours,

[YOUR NAME]
[YOUR TITLE]

Time is Set Request

TO: [*First and last name of person receiving memo*]

FROM: [YOUR NAME]
[YOUR TITLE]

DATE: [DATE]

SUBJECT: [*One or two words defining meeting*] Meeting Scheduled

Internal communications affect external events. Maintaining the highest level of internal communication is essential to any organization's success. As in sports, coaches, trainers, and players alike must thoroughly understand strategies before entering the field.

Likewise, no matter what the purpose of the organization, communication among team members is essential if the team is to have a winning season. There are several new directions regarding [*One or two words defining meeting*] that will influence our business strategies.

This important area for [YOUR COMPANY NAME] warrants your attention and time. There will be a meeting on [*Date of meeting*] in [*Place within office where meeting will be held*] beginning at [*Time the meeting begins*]. Your attendance is essential. Should you be unable to attend, please advise me in writing and include the input you would have provided. Thank you for adding strength to our strategic plays.

cc: [COPIES TO]

Trade Show Announcement

TO: [*First and last name of person receiving memo*]

FROM: [YOUR NAME]
[YOUR TITLE]

DATE: [DATE]

SUBJECT: Trade Show Announcement

Tired of the same old routine? Isn't it time you took action? Seized the opportunity to have customers come to you? Mingled with industry leaders? Or just spent time with your existing accounts away from the telephone?

Get the competitive edge in your marketing and sales future by attending the [*Name of trade show*] on [*Date(s) of trade show*] at [*Building or physical location of trade show in*] in [*City and state of trade show*]. The literature on the event looks like the latest "Who's Who" register in our industry. [YOUR COMPANY NAME] has endorsed *[Name of trade show*] by extending personal invitations to our customers.

For existing customers, the invitation is an act of continued goodwill. New customers are reminded that we haven't forgotten about them. As for prospects, a phone call to invite them provides another opportunity to reaffirm our professional commitment.

Anyone who attends the show will surely walk away with increased market awareness and knowledge of [*Describe the focus of trade show*]. Please prepare a list of your customers who should be invited and outline what will be gained by their attendance. I need this no later than [*Date by which you want to receive name of person receiving invitation*]. Salespeople whose customers are selected to attend the event will be advised.

cc: [COPIES TO]

Trade Show Questionnaire

[DATE]

[Mr./Mrs./Ms./Dr.] [CUSTOMER'S FULL NAME]
[CUSTOMER'S TITLE]
[COMPANY]
[ADDRESS]
[CITY], [STATE] [ZIP CODE]

Dear [Mr./Mrs./Ms./Dr.] [CUSTOMER'S LAST NAME]:

Walking into any trade show, you see them positioned in the doorways. They are the people holding program directories and looking through the index to find a particular company. On the trade show floor, companies are often overshadowed by the banners, booths, crowds, and general hoopla.

Shows such as the one you recently attended, the [*Name of trade show*] on [*Date name of trade show was held*], offer a panoramic view. We hope you'll help us make our next public appearance more beneficial by answering a few short questions.

1. What booth impressed you most at the trade show?

   ____

2. Why did you stop there?

   ____

3. What do you remember about our booth?

   ____

4. Which of the products you saw impressed you most?

   ____

Please return this letter in the enclosed self-addressed, stamped envelope. Thank you for your valuable help in placing our booth in a class by itself. We want every visitor to seek out [YOUR COMPANY NAME]'s company showcase first and last.

Sincerely yours,

[YOUR NAME]
[YOUR TITLE]

Training Seminar

TO: [*First and last name of person receiving memo*]

FROM: [YOUR NAME]
[YOUR TITLE]

DATE: [DATE]

SUBJECT: Expand Your Knowledge of [*Focus of training seminar*] at Training Seminar

When we were younger, most of us thought we knew it all. No one had anything to teach us; we had the answers. With maturity, we realize that there are those who are far more knowledgeable in certain areas.

Calling upon the experts saves us energy and time. [YOUR COMPANY NAME] wants to expand our employees' knowledge of [*Focus of training seminar*]. This not only sustains operations through increased effectiveness, but more important, improves your long-term professional skills.

On [*Date of training seminar*], we have a training seminar planned from [*Time the training seminar begins*] to [*Time the training seminar ends*]. Here, experts will give you information regarding [*List up to three separate points covered in training seminar*]. To reserve your place, please contact [*First and last name of person responsible for R.S.V.P.'s*].

I hope you will recognize the benefits of this training and seize this opportunity to increase your professional skills. The relationship between accomplishment and knowledge stands the test of time. One is dependent on the other for success.

cc: [COPIES TO]

Unauthorized Return

[DATE]

[Mr./Mrs./Ms./Dr.] [CUSTOMER'S FULL NAME]
[CUSTOMER'S TITLE]
[COMPANY]
[ADDRESS]
[CITY], [STATE] [ZIP CODE]

Dear [Mr./Mrs./Ms./Dr.] [CUSTOMER'S LAST NAME]:

We think you'll agree that life would be chaos without rules. Imagine a football game or an airport without them. Clearly, it would be an unpleasant sight.

Similarly, [YOUR COMPANY NAME] abides by rules that guide operations for optimum customer relations and team efficiency. We encourage customers to read the return policy statement found in our [*Name of* YOUR COMPANY NAME *literature in which return policies are located, i.e., "catalog," "contract," etc.*]. When both sides know the rules, potential misunderstandings can be eliminated.

We recently received a [*Name of product returned*] from [COMPANY]. Unfortunately, this return is not in compliance with our policy, because [*Describe in detail why return is not acceptable*]. Therefore, [YOUR COMPANY NAME] cannot provide any credit for the returned goods. If you have any questions or additional information regarding the matter, do not hesitate to contact me. Instant answers are a telephone call away.

Sincerely yours,

[YOUR NAME]
[YOUR TITLE]

Underpayment

[DATE]

[Mr./Mrs./Ms./Dr.] [CUSTOMER'S FULL NAME]
[CUSTOMER'S TITLE]
[COMPANY]
[ADDRESS]
[CITY], [STATE] [ZIP CODE]

Dear [Mr./Mrs./Ms./Dr.] [CUSTOMER'S LAST NAME]:

An error is not a mistake unless it's not corrected. As a well-respected company, [YOUR COMPANY NAME] appreciates opportunities to correct its infrequent errors. We know you follow similar leadership principles.

Unfortunately, the last payment on [COMPANY]'s account was $[*Dollar amount payment was short*] short of the outstanding balance. To prevent finance charges from accruing on the account, please remit $[*Dollar amount payment was short*] no later than [*Date by which* COMPANY *must resubmit payment to* YOUR COMPANY NAME]. Should there be any questions, please do not hesitate to contact us. It will take just a moment to review [COMPANY]'s account activity.

We look forward to the speedy remittance of the outstanding balance. Thank you in advance for your professional handling of this matter. [YOUR COMPANY NAME] assumes that this is merely an oversight.

Sincerely yours,

[YOUR NAME]
[YOUR TITLE]

Urgent Demand

[DATE]

[Mr./Mrs./Ms./Dr.] [CUSTOMER'S FULL NAME]
[CUSTOMER'S TITLE]
[COMPANY]
[ADDRESS]
[CITY], [STATE] [ZIP CODE]

Dear [Mr./Mrs./Ms./Dr.] [CUSTOMER'S LAST NAME]:

[COMPANY] has brought this on itself. On several occasions, [YOUR COMPANY NAME] has politely asked that the debt of $[*Dollar amount of payment needed from* COMPANY] owed to our company be satisfied. Because payment is long overdue, our choices for resolution are severely limited.

Take this notice as a warning, and use your imagination. Think how you would handle this situation if the roles were reversed. Would [COMPANY] continue saying, "Please"? I don't think so.

I do not have to educate you on the importance of credit checks. They are truly an organization's calling card. I recommend that [COMPANY] give the matter immediate attention. If [YOUR COMPANY NAME] has not heard from you by [*Date* COMPANY *must contact* YOUR COMPANY NAME *by*], I will have no choice but to pursue more serious measures. It is my hope that [COMPANY]'s blatant disregard of its debts ends today.

Sincerely yours,

[YOUR NAME]
[YOUR TITLE]

Use of Other Products

[DATE]

[Mr./Mrs./Ms./Dr.] [CUSTOMER'S FULL NAME]
[CUSTOMER'S TITLE]
[COMPANY]
[ADDRESS]
[CITY], [STATE] [ZIP CODE]

Dear [Mr./Mrs./Ms./Dr.] [CUSTOMER'S LAST NAME]:

When entering foreign territory, it's natural for a person to proceed cautiously. We've all learned to test the water before jumping in with both feet. The temperature has to be just right, or at the very least comfortable, to avoid assaulting our senses.

After giving it some thought, I believe this must be the reason [COMPANY] has not given our other superior products a chance. You simply want to be sure [COMPANY] is satisfied with its initial purchases. It's a completely natural thing to do.

Now that you are, I would like to point out some complementary products offered by [YOUR COMPANY NAME]. Have you ever considered how [*Name of a* YOUR COMPANY NAME *product*] would be beneficial to your operations? Or what about [*Name of a* YOUR COMPANY NAME *product different from other product*]? This is merely a small sampling of [YOUR COMPANY NAME]'s portfolio. Enclosed is [*Name of* YOUR COMPANY NAME *literature enclosed with letter, i.e., "brochure," "catalog," etc*] for your browsing pleasure, and additional information is a phone call away. So dive in and take a look; [YOUR COMPANY NAME] has already proven that the water is absolutely perfect!

Sincerely yours,

[YOUR NAME]
[YOUR TITLE]

Vacation Request

TO: [First and last name of person receiving memo]

FROM: [YOUR NAME]
[YOUR TITLE]

DATE: [DATE]

SUBJECT: Vacation Request

Vacations are a necessary evil. I always hesitate to relax and leave projects in process. However, recharging one's batteries away from the office really does wonders.

I am planning a trip [*First day of vacation time*] to [*Last day of vacation time*] using [*Total number of vacation days used*] days of my available vacation time. While figuring out the details, I have noticed that "non-refundable" and "cancellation penalty" are leisure industry buzzwords lately. Therefore, I await your approval before making final arrangements.

Please let me know as soon as possible if my vacation request meets with your approval. Thank you in advance. As you know, "advance bookings" usually net the best prices.

cc: [COPIES TO]

Venture Capital Inquiry

[DATE]

[Mr./Mrs./Ms./Dr.] [FIRST AND LAST NAME]
[TITLE]
[COMPANY]
[ADDRESS]
[CITY], [STATE] [ZIP CODE]

Dear [Mr./Mrs./Ms./Dr.] [LAST NAME]:

The plot of our story is not new: great enterprise shocks marketplace but needs additional funding. Delving beneath the headline, it becomes evident the majority of venture capital criteria have already been satisfied. Your success with other companies in our situation makes this obvious once our whole story is told.

Briefly, [YOUR COMPANY NAME] is on the leading edge of the growing [*Industry* YOUR COMPANY NAME *is in*] industry. An influx of money will determine not if we will grow but, rather, how fast. The funding will be dedicated to [*Describe in an overview why the money is needed*]. After extensive market analysis, additional revenues are within reach.

In order for us to meet our stated objectives, we require an estimated $[*Dollar amount required by* YOUR COMPANY NAME] in the form of either straight financing or joint venture arrangements. However, our company policy requires that a nondisclosure form be signed by an authorized [COMPANY] principal prior to any in-depth discussions. If you are interested in learning more about [YOUR COMPANY NAME], please telephone to arrange delivery of the nondisclosure form. Once you have had an opportunity to review our plans, I am sure you will agree that we have the makings of another American Dream.

Sincerely yours,

[YOUR NAME]

Welcome to Area

[DATE]

[Mr./Mrs./Ms./Dr.] [CUSTOMER'S FULL NAME]
[CUSTOMER'S TITLE]
[COMPANY]
[ADDRESS]
[CITY], [STATE] [ZIP CODE]

Dear [Mr./Mrs./Ms./Dr.] [CUSTOMER'S LAST NAME]:

Moving into a new area is a tough transition. Any change is filled with both apprehension and excitement. It usually has a fresh but sometimes foreign appeal. On behalf of [YOUR COMPANY NAME], I welcome you to this growing community, where our company has prospered and our employees have raised their families for [*Number of years* YOUR COMPANY NAME *has been in business*] years.

[YOUR COMPANY NAME] is filled with friendly faces eager to help with your move. You may be new to our community, but our company's long-standing reputation for superior quality is not. Say [*Describe* YOUR COMPANY NAME's *main business emphasis and what you are trying to market to* COMPANY] around here, and you'll probably hear [YOUR COMPANY NAME].

We are proud of our accomplishments and look forward to welcoming you into our family of customers. Enjoy your new surroundings, and please remember we are here if you ever need [*Describe* YOUR COMPANY NAME's *main business emphasis and what you are trying to market to* COMPANY]. You will be pleased to learn what our customers already know. [YOUR COMPANY NAME] is a reputable company that pays close attention to details and service.

Sincerely yours,

[YOUR NAME]
[YOUR TITLE]

Welcome to New Customer

[DATE]

[Mr./Mrs./Ms./Dr.] [CUSTOMER'S FULL NAME]
[CUSTOMER'S TITLE]
[COMPANY]
[ADDRESS]
[CITY], [STATE] [ZIP CODE]

Dear [Mr./Mrs./Ms./Dr.] [CUSTOMER'S LAST NAME]:

There are 170,000,000,000,000,000,000,000,000 ways to play the opening ten moves in a game of chess. Whether by pawns or knights, the first moves have an enormous impact on the remainder of the match. The same holds true for beginning a business relationship.

I want to make sure our first moves set the stage for mutual respect and trust. It's no secret that you can buy just about anything from someone. We're different, and we're prepared to prove it to you.

It remains my hope that over time, you will recognize how important our business affiliation is to me personally and professionally. Business has been likened many times to a game in which both parties win. I look forward to working together and making the right moves throughout our relationship.

Sincerely yours,

[YOUR NAME]
[YOUR TITLE]

Welcome with Sales Literature

[DATE]

[Mr./Mrs./Ms./Dr.] [CUSTOMER'S FULL NAME]
[CUSTOMER'S TITLE]
[COMPANY]
[ADDRESS]
[CITY], [STATE] [ZIP CODE]

Dear [Mr./Mrs./Ms./Dr.] [CUSTOMER'S LAST NAME]:

Success will never make us so aloof that we forget our manners and fail to extend a welcome. After all, [COMPANY]'s influx of new talent allows our entire community to prosper. [YOUR COMPANY NAME] has been a leading source for [*Describe* YOUR COMPANY NAME's *main business emphasis and what you are trying to market to* COMPANY] in the metropolitan area for years.

Our latest [*Name of* YOUR COMPANY NAME *literature enclosed with letter, i.e., "brochure," "catalog," etc*], which is enclosed, provides an excellent overview of who and what we are. There's much more to the [YOUR COMPANY NAME] story. I could go on for pages listing the numerous ways in which we maintain high levels of customer satisfaction. For now, let's say I would like the opportunity to prove to you what we have proved to others about our company.

Please take a few minutes to examine this information about our company and its offerings. Once you do, I am confident that we will be welcoming you into much more than our community. We will be welcoming you into a family of customers who have found the right source for all their [*Describe* YOUR COMPANY NAME's *main business emphasis and what you are trying to market to* COMPANY] needs.

Sincerely yours,

[YOUR NAME]
[YOUR TITLE]

What Went Wrong?

[DATE]

[Mr./Mrs./Ms./Dr.] [CUSTOMER'S FULL NAME]
[CUSTOMER'S TITLE]
[COMPANY]
[ADDRESS]
[CITY], [STATE] [ZIP CODE]

Dear [Mr./Mrs./Ms./Dr.] [CUSTOMER'S LAST NAME]:

I'm not naive when it comes to business. But, I have trouble understanding what happened. We've called, sent literature, and addressed your concerns, and still you decline to do business with our company. Is there something [YOUR COMPANY NAME] has done wrong?

Many of our customers are just like [COMPANY]. They need [*Describe* YOUR COMPANY NAME's *main business emphasis and what you are trying to market to* COMPANY] with excellent service, and we provide both in the most professional manner. In fact, we've been doing this for our customers for some time now.

There may be other reasons you haven't bought from our company. Perhaps it's just that you're busy and haven't had time to think about how we could work together. If this isn't the case and there are other facts you think I should be aware of, please let me know. It would only help make our respective companies even better.

Sincerely yours,

[YOUR NAME]
[YOUR TITLE]

Whom to Call With Benefits Questions

TO: [*First and last name of person receiving memo*]

FROM: [YOUR NAME]
[YOUR TITLE]

DATE: [DATE]

SUBJECT: Benefits Information Contact

Seeking advice from those without expertise or knowledge is a futile effort. Specialization provides maximum organizational operations. That is why we have dedicated, experienced personnel ready to address any benefits-related questions, comments, or suggestions you may have.

Benefits are more than a plan [YOUR COMPANY NAME] offers to our employees. The entire program demonstrates our total human relations approach, offering employees security in, and out of, the workplace. [*First and last name of person responsible for benefits program*] is eager to serve as a resource and assist with the program's implementation. [*First name of person responsible for benefits program*] can be reached at [*Telephone number for person responsible for benefits program*]. For benefits answers, this is the place.

cc: [COPIES TO]

Work for Hire Agreement

RECITALS:

This is [YOUR COMPANY NAME]'s standard agreement to confirm a Work for Hire arrangement in which we are referred to as "Customer" and [COMPANY] is the "Contractor."

WORK FOR HIRE AGREEMENT

Contractor shall be paid the sum of $[*Cost of—describe and list by number—all work performed by* COMPANY] by Customer for the services described herein. The sum shall be paid upon the timely completion of all of the duties described herein on, or before, [*Date all work is due*]. Contractor agrees to use best efforts to provide [*Describe and list by number of all work performed by* COMPANY] according to the specifications presented by Customer. Contractor shall, at all times, use his or her own tools and employees to complete the terms of this Agreement. Contractor shall not be supervised by Customer but shall proceed to accomplish the task hereunder in whatsoever manner is deemed appropriate within the scope of this Agreement. Customer is aware that Contractor may have other customers and jobs simultaneous with this job. This Agreement does not constitute an employment Agreement, and Contractor shall be considered only as an independent contractor and not as an employee, agent, partner, or joint venturer of Customer. Contractor shall be solely responsible for any and all safety measures and taxes (state, federal, and local); worker's compensation insurance payments; disability payments; social security payments; unemployment insurance payments; other insurance payments; and any similar type of payment for Contractor or any employee thereof, and shall hold Customer harmless from any and all accidents and payments.

Please acknowledge your acceptance of this Work for Hire Agreement by completing the areas below and returning one copy to my attention. Thank you in advance for your assistance.

____

[YOUR NAME]
[YOUR TITLE]

I, [*First and last name of person from* COMPANY *signing*], on behalf of [COMPANY], am authorized to agree to perform the work indicated above under the terms and conditions of this Work for Hire Agreement.

____

Signature

____

Social Security Number

MADE E•Z® LIBRARY

MADE E-Z GUIDES

Each comprehensive guide contains all the information you need to master one of dozens of topics, plus sample forms (if applicable).

Most guides also include an appendix of valuable resources, a handy glossary, and the valuable 14-page supplement "How to Save on Attorney Fees."

ising Your Business Made E-Z G327
the secrets and use the tools of the professionals.

Protection Made E-Z G320
er your property from financial disaster.

ptcy Made E-Z G300
the confusion out of filing bankruptcy.

ss Startups Made E-Z G344
and start any home-based or small business.

/Selling a Business Made E-Z G321
on your business and structure the deal for quick results.

/Selling Your Home Made E-Z G311
r sell your home for the right price—right now.

ing Child Support Made E-Z G315
ce your rights as a single parent.

Repair Made E-Z G303
tools to put you back on track.

Made E-Z G302
ed on your own, without a lawyer.

ment Law Made E-Z G312
dy reference for employers and employees.

ng Your Business Made E-Z G322
ate the best financing and grow your business.

gal Help Made E-Z G339
e your rights—without an expensive lawyer.

uff For Everyone Made E-Z G347
plete roadmap to fabulous freebies.

aising Made E-Z G332
tize big donations with simple ideas.

of Debt Made E-Z
how to become debt-free.

ration Made E-Z G301
ation you need to incorporate your company.

l & Testament Made E-Z G307
will the right way—the E-Z way.

Liability Companies Made E-Z G316
all about the hottest new business entity.

Living Trust Made E-Z G305
Trust us to help you provide for your loved ones.

Living Will Made E-Z G306
Take steps now to insure Death With Dignity.

Marketing Your Small Business Made E-Z G335
Proven marketing strategies for business success.

Money For College Made E-Z G334
Finance your college education—without the debt!

Multi-level Marketing Made E-Z G338
Turn your own product or service into an MLM empire.

Mutual Fund Investing Made E-Z G343
Build a secure future with fast-growth mutual funds.

Offshore Investing Made E-Z G337
Transfer your wealth offshore for financial privacy.

Owning a No-Cash-Down Business Made E-Z G336
Financial independence without risk, cash, or experience.

Partnerships Made E-Z G318
Avoid double taxation.

Profitable Mail Order Made E-Z G323
Turn virtually any product into a profitable mail order item.

SBA Loans Made E-Z G325
In-depth explanation of required and optional forms.

Selling On The Web Made E-Z G324
Wealth-building, web-building strategies for any size business.

Shoestring Investing Made E-Z G330
Amass more wealth with investments through strategic investing.

Stock Market Investing Made E-Z G331
Pick the best stocks and manage your own portfolio.

Solving Business Problems Made E-Z G326
Identify and solve business problems with proven strategies.

Solving IRS Problems Made E-Z G319
Settle with the IRS for pennies on the dollar.

Successful Resumes Made E-Z G346
Exploit your strengths, gain confidence, and secure that dream job.

Winning Business Plans Made E-Z G342
Attract more capital—faster.

Stock No. K307

MADE E•Z® KIT

Each kit includes a clear, concise instructional manual to help y
understand your rights and obligations, plus all the information
and sample forms you need.

*From the leaders in self-help legal products, it's quick, afforda
and it's E-Z.*

$24.95 EACH
(except Last Will and Testament—$19.95)

Stock No. K301

Stock No. K306

...when you need it in writ

Stock No. K311

Stock No. K305

Stock No. K303

Stock No. K316

Stock No. K320

Stock No. K321

Stock No. K302

Stock No. K300

	ITEM #	QTY.	PRICE‡	EXTENSION
E E-Z SOFTWARE				
truction Estimator	SS4300		$29.95	
ractors' Forms	SS4301		$24.95	
rs' Business Builder Bundle	CD325		$59.95	
tection	SS4304		$24.95	
e Records	SS4305		$24.95	
ords	SS4306		$24.95	
l Forms	HR453		$24.95	
ng	SS4308		$24.95	
iability Companies (LLC)	SS4309		$24.95	
ips	SS4310		$24.95	
RS Problems	SS4311		$24.95	
In Small Claims Court	SS4312		$24.95	
g Unpaid Bills	SS4313		$24.95	
n The Web (E-Commerce)	SS4314		$24.95	
itable Home Business	SS4315		$24.95	
ess Lawyer Library	SS4318		$49.95	
Planner	SS4319		$49.95	
nal Lawyer Library	SS4320		$49.95	
	SS4321		$24.95	
Legal Forms and Agreements	SS4322		$24.95	
Legal Forms and Agreements	SS4323		$24.95	
Policies and Manuals	SS4324		$24.95	
tion	SS4333		$24.95	
	SS4327		$24.95	
tartups	SS4332		$24.95	
pair	SW2211		$24.95	
Forms	SW2223		$24.95	
d Selling A Business	SW2242		$24.95	
Your Small Business	SW2245		$24.95	
of Debt	SW2246		$24.95	
Business Plans	SW2247		$24.95	
Resumes	SW2248		$24.95	
isiness Problems	SW 2249		$24.95	
Mail Order	SW2250		$24.95	
siness Forms	SW2251		$49.95	
Business Library	SW2252		$49.95	
onstruction Estimator	SW2253		$19.95	
E E-Z BOOKS				
y	G300		$24.95	
ion	G301		$24.95	
	G302		$24.95	
air	G303		$14.95	
sts	G305		$24.95	
s	G306		$24.95	
Testament	G307		$24.95	
ling Your Home	G311		$14.95	
nt Law	G312		$14.95	
Child Support	G315		$14.95	
bility Companies	G316		$24.95	
os	G318		$24.95	
Problems	G319		$14.95	
ction	G320		$14.95	
ing A Business	G321		$14.95	
Your Business	G322		$14.95	
Mail Order	G323		$14.95	
The Web (E-Commerce)	G324		$14.95	
	G325		$14.95	
siness Problems	G326		$14.95	
Your Business	G327		$14.95	
ing	G328		$14.95	
ath	G329		$14.95	
Investing	G330		$14.95	
t Investing	G331		$14.95	
g	G332		$14.95	
College	G334		$14.95	
our Small Business	G335		$14.95	
o-Cash-Down Business	G336		$14.95	

or a single item, and are subject to change without notice.

MADE E-Z™ PRODUCTS

TO PLACE AN ORDER:

1. Duplicate this order form.
2. Complete your order and mail or fax to:

Made E-Z Products

384 S. Military Trail

Deerfield Beach, FL 33442

www.MadeE-Z.com

Tel: 954-480-8933

Toll Free: 800-822-4566

Fax: 954-480-8906

continued on next page

	ITEM #	QTY.	PRICE‡	EXTENSION
Offshore Investing	G337		$14.95	
Multi-level Marketing	G338		$14.95	
Free Legal Help	G339		$14.95	
Get Out Of Debt	G340		$14.95	
Winning Business Plans	G342		$14.95	
Mutual Fund Investing	G343		$14.95	
Business Startups	G344		$14.95	
Successful Resumes	G346		$14.95	
Free Stuff For Everyone	G347		$14.95	
On-Line Business Resources	G348		$14.95	
Life Insurance	G349		$14.95	
Health Insurance	G350		$14.95	
Successful Selling	G351		$14.95	
Everyday Legal Forms & Agreements	BK407		$24.95	
Personnel Forms	BK408		$24.95	
Collecting Unpaid Bills	BK409		$24.95	
Corporate Records	BK410		$24.95	
Everyday Law	BK411		$24.95	
Vital Records	BK412		$24.95	
Business Forms	BK414		$24.95	
MADE E-Z KITS				
Bankruptcy Kit	K300		$24.95	
Incorporation Kit	K301		$24.95	
Divorce Kit	K302		$24.95	
Credit Repair Kit	K303		$24.95	
Living Trust Kit	K305		$24.95	
Living Will Kit	K306		$24.95	
Last Will & Testament Kit	K307		$19.95	
Buying and Selling Your Home Kit	K311		$24.95	
Business Startups Kit	K320		$24.95	
Small Business/Home Business Kit	K321		$24.95	
MISC. PRODUCTS				
☆ Federal Labor Law Poster	LP001		$5.99	
☆ State Specific Labor Law Poster (see state listings below)			$29.95	
E-Z Legal Will Pac	WP250		$9.95	

State	Item#	QTY
AL	83801	
AK	83802	
AZ	83803	
AR	83804	
CA	83805	
CO	83806	
CT	83807	
DE	83808	
DC	83848	
FL	83809	
GA	83810	
HI	83811	
ID	83812	
IL	83813	
IN	83814	
IO	83815	

State	Item#	QTY
KY	83817	
LA	83818	
ME	83819	
MD	83820	
MA	83821	
MI	83822	
MN	83823	
MS	83824	
MO	83825	
MT	83826	
NE	83827	
NV	83828	
NH	83829	
NJ	83830	
NM	83831	
NY	83832	

State	Item#	QTY
ND	83834	
OH	83835	
OK	83836	
OR	83837	
PA	83838	
RI	83839	
SC	83840	
S. Dakota not available		
TN	83842	
TX	83843	
UT	83844	
VT	83845	
VA	83846	
WA	83847	
WV	83849	
WI	83850	

ORDER TOTAL ☆ Required by Federal & State Laws	$
SHIPPING & HANDLING $4.95 for first item, $1.50 for each additional item *All orders shipped Ground unless otherwise specified.*	$
SUBTOTAL	$
Florida Residents add 6% sales tax	$
TOTAL	$

‡ Prices are for a single item, and are subject to change without notice.

MADE E-Z™ PRODUCTS

Name

Company

Address

City

State Zip

Phone
( )

PAYMENT METHOD:

❑ Charge my credit card:
❑ MasterCard
❑ VISA
❑ American Express

❑ Check enclosed, payable to:
Made E-Z Products
384 S. Military Trail
Deerfield Beach, FL 33442

ACCOUNT NO. EXP D

Signature:

(required for credit card purchases)

Company Purchase Orders Ar
Welcome With Approved Credi

Comments & Suggestion

Thank you

Index of Forms

-A-

-B-

-D-

-E-

-J-

-L-

-M-

-N-